D1242431

devotions for you and your friends

True Beauty

THE INSIDE STORY

Andrea Stephens

Regal

From Gospel Light
Ventura, California, U.S.A.

PUBLISHED BY REGAL BOOKS
FROM GOSPEL LIGHT
VENTURA, CALIFORNIA, U.S.A.
PRINTED IN THE U.S.A.

Regal Books is a ministry of Gospel Light, a Christian publisher dedicated to serving the local church. We believe God's vision for Gospel Light is to provide church leaders with biblical, user-friendly materials that will help them evangelize, disciple and minister to children, youth and families.

It is our prayer that this Regal book will help you discover biblical truth for your own life and help you meet the needs of others. May God richly bless you.

For a free catalog of resources from Regal Books/Gospel Light, please call your Christian supplier or contact us at 1-800-4-GOSPEL *or* www.regalbooks.com.

Originally published by Servant Publications in 2000.

Scripture quotations are from
NASB—Scripture taken from the *New American Standard Bible,* © 1960, 1962, 1963, 1968, 1971, 1972, 1973, 1975, 1977 by The Lockman Foundation. Used by permission.
NIV—Scripture taken from the *Holy Bible, New International Version*®. Copyright © 1973, 1978, 1984 by International Bible Society. Used by permission of Zondervan Publishing House. All rights reserved.
NRSV—The Scripture quotations contained herein are from the *New Revised Standard Version Bible,* copyright 1989, by the Division of Christian Education of the National Council of the Churches of Christ in the U.S.A. Used by permission. All rights reserved.
TLB—Scripture quotations marked (*TLB*) are taken from *The Living Bible,* copyright © 1971. Used by permission of Tyndale House Publishers, Inc., Wheaton, IL 60189. All rights reserved.

© 2000 Andrea Stephens
All rights reserved.

Cover photo © John Henley / The Stock Market. Used by permission.

Library of Congress Cataloging-in-Publication Data
(Applied for)

ISBN: 0-8307-3509-7

1 2 3 4 5 6 7 8 9 10 11 12 13 14 15 / 10 09 08 07 06 05 04

Rights for publishing this book in other languages are contracted by Gospel Light Worldwide, the international nonprofit ministry of Gospel Light. Gospel Light Worldwide also provides publishing and technical assistance to international publishers dedicated to producing Sunday School and Vacation Bible School curricula and books in the languages of the world. For additional information, visit www.gospellightworldwide.org; write to Gospel Light Worldwide, P.O. Box 3875, Ventura, CA 93006; or send an e-mail to info@gospellightworldwide.org.

This book is dedicated to...

The precious women in my life who have awed me over the years with their breathtaking (and mind-boggling) display of the beautiful qualities of the Holy Spirit. Your examples have been both a blessing in my life and an encouragement for me to keep abiding in the Vine, just as you have. I pray my fruit will ripen to be as sweet as yours.

I also pray that God will grant in the life of each young woman who reads this book the ability and desire to become a godly woman who will be a living example of the Spirit-filled life.

Contents

How to Use This Book to Become Beautiful

I don't know about you, but I've always wanted to be beautiful. I thought it would be impossible until I discovered the meaning of beauty as defined by the ultimate expert in the beauty business—God! I discovered that being truly attractive was not about our hips and hairdos, but about our hearts! Each of us has the potential to become the blessed owner of a beautiful heart that will guarantee our status as a TRUE BEAUTY! That's what this book is all about!

The first chapter will introduce the nine beautiful qualities (fruits) of the Holy Spirit and explain how we can develop them in our lives. The next nine chapters contain five daily devotions that will explore each beauty quality. On day one, we'll define it. Day two will observe the opposite. On day three, we'll see how Jesus portrays it. Day four will tell how a female Bible character expressed it in her life. Then on day five, you'll have the opportunity to take a quiz to help you determine where you are with each quality.

Each daily devotional has two parts: the reading itself, followed by the Beauty Builders. These are loaded with great questions that will help you think through the main points of the day and see how they apply to your life. Cool.

Each chapter closes with a writing assignment called Weekend Journal. This will give you a chance to jot down your thoughts, feelings, and prayers.

Since the Lord desires for you to demonstrate his beautiful qualities every day, you will be able to apply what you are learning right away.

You can rest assured that these are long-lasting beauty qualities that won't go out of fashion or change with each new season. Being beautiful is totally possible. Let's get started!

Chapter One

Born to Be Beautiful!

*The Beautiful Qualities
of the Holy Spirit*

Heavenly Handiwork

"True beauty lives in the heart."
Abbie, 16

OK, I'll admit it. When I was in high school I spent more time studying fashion magazines than studying math. That's because I wanted what *they* had. Flawless skin. Almond-shaped eyes. Full, bouncy hair. Pearly white teeth. A firm tush. A tall, thin body.

You see, that's what our culture says it takes to be beautiful!

But wait. Take a look at the girls in the lunch line, check out the co-chicks in your classes. Do they look like super-model material? Nope! That's 'cause less than 1 percent of our population has the so-called *right* physical characteristics to be considered beautiful.

Then why did you title this section "Born To Be Beautiful!"? I can just hear you tossing that question my way. And I am 100 percent prepared to toss the answer right back!

I am convinced that you were BORN TO BE BEAUTIFUL! Listen up, here comes the explanation. You were born to be beautiful according to *God's* definition of beauty, not our culture's. Not Hollywood's!

If God were to jot down his requirements for a girl to be on his list of the world's Top Ten Beautiful Babes, there would not be a single reference to looks. It's true. In God's book, the Bible, physical appearance is not part of what makes a person beautiful.

That's because in God's eyes we are ALL beautiful! He is the one who created and designed each one of us. Just like the master sculptor who works with the clay until it looks exactly the way he wants it to look, so God has handcrafted you and me.

God already thinks we are outrageously gorgeous. He loves what we see when we look in the mirror! That's right. I'm saying that no matter what you look like—small, squinty eyes, wide nose, thick waistline, bony knees, flat hair—in God's opinion (and it's a pretty powerful, valuable opinion, I might point out), YOU have a heavenly appearance. You are fine! You are divine! God looks down and says, "She's mine!"

I'll give you a minute to chew on that. Now that you've swallowed it, consider this.

God's designs are totally perfect. He doesn't mess up. What he creates is exactly what he intends to create.

And the best part about it is this: God loves his creation. God loves you. God loves me. We are equally attractive to him. None of that Laura's-got-better-hair-than-Susie or Karen-is-not-as-proportioned-as-Becky stuff with God.

He doesn't determine our beauty by seeing how we measure up to one another. In fact, he purposely chose to create each of us differently. You and I are one-of-a-kind designs. That's too cool. And like a true artist, who has completed the final handiwork, God steps back, gives you the once-over, and smiles. Just looking at you brings joy to the Father's heart.

What? You don't believe I'm being straight with you? You don't like what you see in the mirror and can't believe God likes it either? You constantly compare yourself to others and think that on a scale of one to ten you're a subzero? Check out my book, *God Thinks You're Positively Awesome,* to get the stereophonic scoop on this topic!

Sometimes we are easily swayed to accept what we see around

us as truth. The world's beauty message is loud and clear. We see it and hear it everywhere we go. But I believe God's truth always wins out.

I encourage you to forget what you see with your eyes and hear with your ears. Instead, look into God's Word and listen with your heart to his teachings. There you will discover real truth. There you will find the key to true beauty.

Beauty Builders

1. God created and designed you! But don't take my word for it. Read it for yourself in Psalm 139:13-16 and Isaiah 64:8. How does it feel knowing you are handmade? Why should you avoid comparing yourself with others?

2. Our world knows how to pour on the pressure. Yet, Romans 12:2 instructs us to be new and different—refusing to copy the ways of the world. Give it a read, then write down the pressures you have felt to fit the world's beauty mold. What can you and your friends do to relieve the pressure?

Day Two

The Make-Over

God desires that we would be beautiful on the inside! That's why he's not hung up on physical beauty. He has something far more important on his mind. It's your heart! People might look at the outward appearance, but the Lord doesn't (see 1 Samuel 16:7). Listen to this:

> *Don't be concerned about the outward beauty that depends on jewelry, or beautiful clothes, or hair arrangement. Be beautiful inside, in your hearts, with the lasting charm of a gentle and quiet spirit which is so precious to God.*
>
> 1 PETER 3:3-4, TLB

Wow! True beauty is not displayed on the outside. It's on the inside!

And here you thought you needed to skip meals, work out, fix your 'do, load on the makeup, shop at Old Navy, and eventually get implants and liposuction!

No way, girlfriend!

Real beauty is not about being zit-free or fat-free. It's not about the labels you proudly wear on your backside. True beauty is all about the inside.

God wants you to have a beautiful heart! That's great, but where do you get one? Is there a store running specials on them? Nope. So, how can you have a lovely heart that will be precious to God?

Enter Holy Spirit! Yep! This is where the Holy Spirit comes in. He is the one who helps out in the heart department. Hang with me and we'll find out how.

Do you recall the story that precedes the world's most famous Bible verse, John 3:16? Jesus is explaining to Nicodemus (a Jewish leader) that in order to enter the kingdom of God, he must be born again. To be born again simply means that you invite Jesus into your life to be your Savior (the one who forgives you of your sins and saves you from eternal punishment) and your Lord (the one who sits in the driver's seat of your life).

When you do this, a very significant miracle occurs. God sends the Holy Spirit to live inside of you!

As Jesus explained, it's not your body that is reborn, it's your spirit. The inner person of your heart is made new. And when the Holy Spirit himself comes to make his home in you, you become a TRUE BEAUTY!

And being as special as he is, the Holy Spirit brings with him some very special characteristics that will cause you to grow and develop into the beautiful woman God desires you to be.

Flip open to Galatians 5:22. What are the nine qualities or fruits of the Holy Spirit? Love, joy, peace, patience, kindness, goodness, faithfulness, gentleness, and self-control! When we allow the Holy Spirit to flow through our lives, these qualities will be evident. They are not just the fruit of the Spirit, they are the PROOF of the Spirit living in us.

Do you want to know more about these nine qualities? Want to know exactly how they are to be played out in your life? Want to learn about some women of the Bible who had beautiful hearts?

What about Jesus? Want to know if he demonstrated these qualities in his life? If so, you came to the right place. That's exactly what the rest of this book is about. Keep reading!

You have the potential to become the proud owner of a beautiful heart that will guarantee your status as a TRUE BEAUTY!

Beauty Builders

1. Reread 1 Peter 3:3-4. Have you been more concerned about your outside than your inside? How does being more concerned about your outward appearance take your focus away from developing a beautiful heart?

2. So, the Holy Spirit lives inside of believers? Absolutely! Get the full scoop in John 14:16-17 and 1 Corinthians 6:19-20. Does knowing that the Holy Spirit lives in you make you aware of changes you need to make in your lifestyle? If so, list what they are and create a plan of action to change them.

Opening Your Heart

The first step toward real beauty is opening your heart to the Lord and inviting the Holy Spirit to live in and through you. If you have never done that, please pray with me today.

Dear Heavenly Father,
I believe that you are God, the Creator of all things, including me! I realize my heart will never be beautiful until you send the Holy Spirit to live in me. So, I open the door of my heart. I ask that your Son, Jesus, would forgive me of my sins, and that your Spirit would come make his home in me today—right now.

Thank you, Father, that I am now reborn to be beautiful! Fill me with your beautiful qualities that my life might be a blessing to you and to those around me. In Jesus' name, Amen.

Signed:_____Date:_____

Gorgeous Girl Profile
Miss Natalie Lloyd
The Girl With the Beautiful Heart

Poke your head into the drama room and you might see her rehearsing for the new school play or practicing for an upcoming oratorical contest. At church you can find her laughing with delight as she hangs up projects created by the fourth- and fifth-grade Sunday school class she teaches. Or you may catch her interviewing her youth group friends about their visit to the local nursing home (yep, she's the editor of the youth newsletter, *The Light*).

In her spare time she enjoys recording books on tape for physically and mentally challenged children. And just for fun, she collects stuffed sheep—a reminder to her that God is the Good Shepherd and we are the precious sheep that he loves.

Who is she? Natalie Lloyd, the 1999 Brio Girl!

Every year *Brio* magazine (published by Focus on the Family) searches for a girl who cares about others, her family, and her schoolwork, and who is growing in her relationship with the Lord. Among the thousands of applicants each year, there are lots of great girls who would qualify.

But there was something that kept drawing the judges back to Natalie.

It was her heart. They began referring to her as the girl with the beautiful heart. It was evident in the way she answered the questions and the activities in which she was involved. Her videotape revealed a gentle love that shone through her eyes and through her smile. She had a heart that glowed with a beauty from within.

Standing only 4'11" and walking with a slight limp, Natalie has endured a lifelong struggle with Osteogenesis Imperfecta. She has broken her legs more than fifteen times, resulting in numerous surgeries, being wheelchair-bound, needing a walker or a cane, and months of rehab.

Growing up, Natalie was unable to run, jump, or play with the other kids. Even now she can't play basketball, water-ski, or go out for the track team. To some, it would appear that Natalie is always on the sidelines of life.

Not true. God's game plan for her is just different.

Natalie says, "Even when I was little, God used my disability as a platform for his love. I didn't let my problem get me down; instead I found an ultimate peace in someone who had plans for *me specifically,* regardless of the physical challenges before me. I've learned that by leaning on God, he can continually guide my paths and strengthen my walk, for 'His strength is made perfect in my weakness'" (2 Corinthians 12:9).

Now *that's* a beautiful heart!

Day Three

Plugged In!

Kaylea was losing her race against time. Her English paper kept her up past midnight, causing her to sleep through her morning alarm. Forget showering. Forget washing her hair. She had time for only a little mascara, lip gloss, and a quick touch-up on her bangs. She would just throw the rest of her hair in a scrunchee. As long as her bangs were right, she'd be OK.

Rushing into the bathroom, Kaylea grabbed her curling iron. Oh, no! She had turned it on five minutes ago, but had forgotten to PLUG IT IN!

A curling iron cannot heat up and do what it is designed to do unless it is plugged into the power source.

The same is true for us. Unless we are connected or plugged into our power source, the Holy Spirit will have a tough time leading us to do what we are designed to do—to have a beautiful heart that is so full of love, joy, peace, and patience that it spills over onto others.

As kids of the King, when we stay connected to Christ, the Holy Spirit has the power to work in our lives. Our job is to stay connected. The Bible refers to this as abiding in the Vine. Abiding means to remain, to dwell, or to live within! It's like pitching your tent and settling in. We are to connect up to Christ and stay there! Jesus said:

> *Abide in me, and I in you. As the branch cannot bear fruit of itself, unless it abides in the vine, so neither can you, unless you abide in me. I am the vine, you are the branches; he who abides in me, and I in him, he bears much fruit; for apart from me you can do nothing.*

> JOHN 15:4-5, NASB

Obviously, abiding in Christ is incredibly important! So how do we do it? Jesus gives us a hint when he says, "If you abide in my word, then you are truly disciples of mine" (John 8:31, NASB). OK, that's more than a hint! It's an absolute giveaway!

Abide in his Word! Plug into the Bible on a regular basis.

When you do this, your mind will get renewed (see Romans 12:2), and you will discover a whole new way to think and live. Putting God's Word in your mind will teach you how to live in a way that is pleasing to God. Life starts to change. New desires, attitudes, and actions take root and begin to grow in your heart. You desire to please God with the thoughts you choose to think, the words you choose to say, and the actions you choose to take.

As you abide in the Vine, you become more aware of the Holy Spirit's presence inside of you. You begin to understand that it isn't YOU living your life anymore but it is Christ living in you. You truly develop the desire to ask what Jesus would do, and, when you get the answer, you do it.

Abiding in the Vine gives you the desire and strength to *choose* to behave in a godly way. Choose to be loving, joyful, peaceful, patient, kindhearted, good, faithful, gentle, and to have self-control. You choose to work hand in hand with the Holy Spirit to produce a beautiful heart.

Wait, did I say *choose*? Don't these nine qualities just come naturally now that the Holy Spirit lives in you? Eventually perhaps, but in the beginning there's a BATTLE going on! Something is trying to steal your beauty! Join me tomorrow for all the juicy details!

Beauty Builders

1. Check out John 15:1-6. What happens to a branch that disconnects itself from the vine and doesn't bear fruit? How can you keep this from happening to you?

2. Read John 15:8 and fill in the blanks. When you produce fruit in your life it glorifies _____ and proves you are a _____ of Jesus! Do you need to spend more time abiding in the Vine? Do you need to produce more spiritual fruit? Does your life prove you are a believer?

Six Ways to Abide in God's Word

1. *Read It!* Have a daily Bible reading time, whether it's five chapters or five verses! Buy a study guide or commentary to help you discover the full meaning of the Word. You will strengthen your relationship with God and tighten your grip on the Vine in a BIG way. (Remember, God's Word is spiritually charged and empowered to change us and fill us with the qualities of the Holy Spirit.) Let the word of Christ dwell in you richly (COLOSSIANS 3:16, NIV).

2. *Hear It!* Hearing God's Word builds our faith (see Romans 10:17), which keeps us abiding in the Vine. When you attend church, Sunday school, youth group, listen to Christian radio or TV, or even read the Bible out loud to yourself, you will be *hearing* the Word!

---

3. Memorize It! Hide God's Word in your heart by meditating on it and memorizing it. That's real abiding—allowing the Word to live inside of you. Write the verses you want to memorize on 3 X 5 cards and hang them up or make yourself a set of flash cards. Break the verses into segments and memorize a piece at a time. You can do it! You can join the psalmist in saying, "I have hidden your word in my heart that I might not sin against you" (Psalm 119:11, NIV). Then when you get in a situation and need to hear from the Lord, he will draw that verse up out of your memory and use it to lead you.

4. Obey It! That's right. Be a *doer* of the Word (see James 1:22). Obedience proves your love for God and reaps spiritual blessings in your life. Obeying the Word also makes it more real in your life; it becomes a deep part of you. Disobedience (sin) breaks your fellowship with God. That's the opposite of abiding!

5. Pray It! Yep! Incorporate Scripture verses into your prayers. This is easily done if you have studied and memorized God's Word. For example, if you need peace, you could pray using Philippians 4:7: "Lord, I ask you to give me your peace, the kind that is more wonderful than I can imagine, the kind that will quiet my heart and my mind as I trust in you." Praying God's Word packs a new power in your prayer life!

6. Sing It! Listening to tapes or CDs of artists that use lyrics based on God's Word will help you keep your mind focused on him. It will help you resist temptations throughout the day so you can live a godly life. For a double blessing, grab your Walkman and go out for a "praise walk"! "Sing psalms, hymns and spiritual songs with gratitude in your hearts to God" (Colossians 3:16, NIV).

Day Four

Winning the Beauty Battle

Whenever there's a battle, there are two opposing teams. Two sides trying to get their own way. Two competitors fighting to win. The same is true in the beauty battle!

For instance, pretend your best friend—let's call her Anna—was just nominated for homecoming court and you weren't. You know that reacting joyfully and celebrating this exciting moment in her life would be the more attractive way to respond.

But, instead, you are plagued with pangs of jealousy and are tempted to snub Anna the next time you see her in the hall.

Feel the tug of war? Do you sense the inner struggle? Who will win? Do you show the beautiful quality of joy or the ugly feeling of jealousy?

With the Holy Spirit on your side, you have a powerful new strength available to help you choose to be a beautiful you.

But what about those ugly thoughts and feelings? Those yucky desires? Where do they come from? How do you get rid of them? How do you win the beauty battle?

Those unattractive attitudes and actions are our evil inclinations and wrongful desires that come from what the Bible calls our flesh. F for fickle, L for lustful, E for evil, S for selfish, H for horrible! FLESH!

Our flesh, which we have to live in every day, was used to getting its own way and acting however it pleased. But then the Holy Spirit showed up, and the battle began! The Holy Spirit always leads us to behave in a godly fashion, while the flesh urges us to let *ugly* rule. What the flesh wants is always opposite of what the Spirit wants.

Fear not! The Spirit in you *wins* as you abide in the Vine and are obedient to his prompting. The Holy Spirit helps you to know the right way to act, but you have to choose to do it. When you take up sides with the Holy Spirit and step out in faith to do or say what would be pleasing to God, the Spirit will fill you with his supernatural strength to follow through.

Laura found this to be true one day after a conference basketball game. She was about to let her angry words spill out all over Dee, the point guard, whose major mess-up cost them the game. But she quickly asked the Holy Spirit to give her the self-control she needed to keep her mouth shut. He did. She did!

Like Laura, ask the Holy Spirit to give you what you need when you need it.

With the bold and beautiful power of God's Spirit in you, you can choose love over hate, joy over jealousy, peace over strife, patience over impatience, kindness over revenge, goodness over evil, faithfulness over quitting, gentleness over rudeness, and self-control over doing whatever feels good at the moment!

The Bible tells us to live by the Spirit and we will not give in to the ugly desires of our flesh (see Galatians 5:16). It's true! Our desire to please God has to override our desire to please our flesh or ourselves. Keep submitting yourself to the control of the Holy Spirit in your life and don't allow your flesh to do just any old unattractive thing it wants.

Wait! Does that mean acting patient or being faithful even when you don't *feel* like it? Yep. Being faithful is not based on feeling, it's based on obedience! Besides, when you do something you don't feel like doing, you are using the fruit of self-control.

Oh, yes, there will be times when you let your flesh win! But that puts the brakes on inner beauty. It keeps the Spirit from shining through you, and it dulls your relationship with the Lord. So, quickly apologize to the Lord and get back on track!

Whatever you do, never give up! Refuse to wave the white flag of surrender. Don't get frustrated and toss in the towel. You are growing in your life with the Spirit, learning to walk hand in hand with him. Growth takes time. And tomorrow it's time to talk about it. You are in a beauty-building process!

Beauty Builders

1. Take a closer look at the big bad flesh who tries to flex his muscles and intimidate the Holy Spirit. Read Galatians 5:19-21. Record the sinful deeds of the flesh. Then, grab a dictionary and define each deed. In which of these areas do you struggle?

2. On the flip side of the flesh is the Spirit. Review the fruits or characteristics of the Holy Spirit in Galatians 5:22-23. Which of these are most challenging to you and why?

Day Five

Growing More Gorgeous Every Day

In the beautiful heart business, there is no such thing as an overnight success. True beauty takes time. True beauty is lasting. God fills you with his Spirit, who brings to you the beautiful qualities of love, joy, peace, patience, kindness, goodness, faithfulness, gentleness, and self-control.

Because you know God wants you to display these incredible characteristics, you choose to act accordingly. As you continue to stay closely connected to God by reading his Word, praying, and memorizing Scripture, the most amazing thing happens. Really, it does!

Instead of having to stop and make the decision to act kind or choose to be patient, those Spirit-filled responses begin to come more naturally. (See, ultimately it's not about trying harder, it's about abiding deeper.)

That is the result of the growth process at work in our lives.

Let's use Jesus' example of the vine and the branches to get a clear glimpse of how the Holy Spirit works in our lives to make us so lovely.

In the vineyard, there is a vinedresser. He is the one who cares for the vineyard, providing everything it needs to produce a beautiful harvest. God, as our Father, is our Vinedresser. He is the one who oversees the growth in our lives. He brings into our lives the circumstances and situations we need to cause us to grow closer to him and develop Christlike character.

Jesus is the Vine. We are the branches. In order for a branch to grow and produce luscious fruit, it must be attached to the vine. So we must stay connected to Jesus. We must remain linked to the Lord.

It is important that we don't run off with every distraction or be pulled away from Jesus by every temptation that comes our way. The secret drive to be popular, fit in with the crowd, or be accepted can steer us off track. Even good activities like sports, service clubs, and extracurricular activities can pull us away from our time with the Lord and disconnect us from the Vine.

And it's from the vine that flows the nourishment the branch needs to grow. That's the Holy Spirit! He is the life-giving source that flows from God, through Jesus, to us.

Back to the branch. Soon, the small buds that have appeared on the branch break open, allowing the tightly curled, green leaves to peek out and unfold in the sunlight! Then tiny white blossoms with a fragrant aroma appear on the branch. Ah! Proof that fruit is on its way!

As we begin to love the Lord and his Word more fully, we, too, give off a fragrant aroma (see 2 Corinthians 2:14-15). We smell great! And, our willingness to say yes to the Holy Spirit's prompting to be good, gentle, and loving is proof that we will eventually produce a full harvest of beauty as we continue to grow.

After a while, the blossom fades and tiny nubs appear at the end of the branch. After months and months of sunlight, water, fertilizer, and proper care, those nubs develop into deliciously ripe, mature grapes. Yummy fruit. So soft and so sweet! The fruit cannot be fully enjoyed until it's truly ripe.

As the Holy Spirit's characteristics grow in us, we go through various stages. Sometimes it feels like we'll never be truly attractive on the inside. Not true. In Ecclesiastes 3:11 God promises that he makes everything beautiful in his own time. Your job is to abide in the Vine. God's job is to cause you to blossom into a beautiful young woman. Look out! Outrageously attractive is just around the corner!

Beauty Builders

1. Check out the three requests in David's incredible prayer by reading Psalm 27:4. (To dwell in God's house means to live in his presence; to behold the beauty of the Lord means to keep your eyes fixed on him—observing him and his ways, and purposing in your heart to be like him; to meditate in his temple means to contemplate his goodness and faithfulness.)

   Can you honestly request the same things David did? Write a letter to God, personalizing David's prayer.

2. Satan does not want us to abide in the Vine. He hates it when we grow in the Lord. He has some specific tactics to try to cut us off from Jesus. Read Mark 4:1-20 and 1 John 2:15-16. List the things that distract us from abiding in the Word and cause us to become disinterested in living the Christian life. How can you avoid each of these things in your life?

Weekend Journal

Write a letter to God telling him the most important thing you learned this week about developing a beautiful heart, why it's important, and what impact this discovery will have on your life. Follow this with a prayer asking him to help you become more beautiful on the inside.

Dear Heavenly Father,

With love,

_____

Chapter Two

Alluringly Adorable!

*The Beautiful Quality
of Love*

This Thing Called Love

"Genuine love is a constant commitment proven by our actions instead of our words."
Stephanie, 18

Cindy flipped open her suitcase. Spending the weekend with Lisa's family at their beach house was going to be so cool. As she scanned her room, she saw all of the stuff she wanted to be sure to pack.

Oh, I LOVE this new CD; that's gotta go, she thought. Into the suitcase it went. Holding up her two favorite swimsuits, she decided on the two-piece. *I LOVE the way I look in this, plus, I adore this print.* In it went. She couldn't forget her hair gel. *I LOVE the wet look I get with this gel—it's a must for the beach.* She snuggled it in next to her jammies.

All packed and ready to go, Cindy kissed her mom and dad at the door and headed out to join Lisa's family in their van. She turned, waved, and yelled, "Oh, I love you guys." Her parents smiled.

Love. It's a word in the English language that holds lots of different meanings. Cindy loved her CD. She loved her two-piece bathing suit. And she loved her parents. But did she love them all the same way? To the same degree? Of course not! Yet, she used the same word in all situations!

The Greek language, the one in which the New Testament was originally written, uses three different words to describe love.

Philos means friendship or brotherly love. *Eros* refers to intense physical or sexual-type love (hey, this word is not even *used* in the New Testament!). And the third is the big one ... *agape!*

Agape love is so incredible! It's unconditional—no strings attached. It's unselfish—totally giving. It's unending—it never stops. It's forgiving—no grudges here! It's a love that is based on commitment, not wishy-washy feelings. It's a God-kind of love!

The word *agape* is used throughout the New Testament to teach us how to love the way God loves. See, love is a huge deal to God. It's the very core of who he is and who he wants us to be. For two reasons, it's listed as the first quality the Holy Spirit builds in us.

First, love gets top billing with Jesus. He tells us to love others as he has loved us. It is to be the ruling and motivating force in our lives. Everything Jesus did and said was in love. He desires we would do the same.

Second, love is the word that sums up all the other beauty qualities! The other eight—joy, peace, patience, kindness, goodness, faithfulness, gentleness, and self-control—are all based on love. It's like a big grapefruit! The whole fruit represents love. When you peel it, you can then see the individual segments inside. Each segment represents a beauty quality, but all of them together make up the whole grapefruit—or love! Get it?

Contrary to what you see portrayed on TV and in the movies, genuine love is not about candlelight dinners, boxes of candy, bundles of roses, flip-flop feelings in your tummy, or passionate acts of sex.

The Bible describes agape love in 1 Corinthians 13. This description of love is Holy Spirit–empowered! It's beyond what we can muster up on our own. The Holy Sprit working in us helps us to love in this supernatural style. Real love is energized by the ever-present Holy Spirit.

Want to be truly beautiful? Learn to love with absolute agape!

Beauty Builders

1. Cindy made no distinction between agape love and the other types of love. Have you thought about the different meanings of love? How have you demonstrated agape love to someone in your life?

2. Let's discover the special ingredients that define genuine love. Read 1 Corinthians 13. Now zero in on verses 1-3. Exactly how important is genuine love? Explain.

3. There are fifteen incredible descriptions of love in verses 4-8. Choose two of them you'd like to work on this week and tell how you plan to do it.

Day Two

Selfishness ... the Beauty Squelcher

Agape love, the God kind of love, is totally selfless. It's all about giving, not getting.

Therefore, the opposite of genuine love would be selfishness. Selfishness is about a girl's heart that has grown cold and focuses on *her* wants, *her* desires, *her* needs. Forget others. They're not *her* problem. A selfish heart is far from beautiful.

Take a look at Liz. You'll see what I mean. Liz lived in the cold, dark shadow of someone she considered a huge monster—her older sister Lauren. Lauren was sort of a Miss Everything at their high school. She usually aced her exams and actually liked writing those dreadful English papers. Her science project was a major success, and she was written up in the school newspaper.

Lauren had a winsome and warm personality. She was quick with a smile and had tons of friends. And it didn't matter what she wore. Even her track uniform looked great on her!

Liz was beside herself with envy most of the time. She wanted everything Lauren had. She wanted to be smart and liked and stylish and athletic. Her selfish heart was so crowded, storing up those rotten thoughts about her older sibling.

Liz's selfishness soon turned to jealousy. She despised her sister and wished they didn't have to breathe the same air! Jealousy gave way to hatred, which took root in her heart, and she began to look for an opportunity to cut Lauren down to size.

Her scheming mind went to work, and it didn't take long to conjure up the perfect plan for her dirty deed.

Lauren had been selected by the faculty to present her senior paper in front of the entire student body. It was sixteen pages long—no way could it be memorized. *Perfect*, thought Liz.

The night before the big event, Liz erased Lauren's paper from the family PC. And after Lauren had gone to bed, Liz swiped her paper and hid it in the living room under a sofa cushion. She could hardly sleep, thinking about how gratifying it would be to see Lauren fall flat on her face!

Liz's heart was far from attractive! Selfishness led to jealousy. Jealousy opened the door to hatred. Hatred allowed vengeance to step right in and take action. The results were ugly.

Are you or someone you know suffering from this condition? Are you in need of a little spiritual heart surgery? Is there hope for an icy-cold, selfish heart?

Yep!

How?

By digging your roots deeper!

Huh?

A selfish heart is an indication of a shallow heart. Ephesians 3:17 says that we are to be rooted and grounded in love. If our roots are shallow, we'll buckle when the heat's on. We'll give in to feelings of selfishness. God desires that our roots would go down deep in the soil of his incredible love.

When our roots are deep in Christ and we honestly realize how much God loves us, then we can draw from him what we need to love others. The more time we spend with the Lord, the more love we will have to splash around on others. God's love can overpower our temptation to be selfish. Yep! With the Holy Spirit's help, we can change selfish to selfless. Details coming up tomorrow!

Beauty Builders

1. A cold, selfish heart will melt in the presence of God's love. Go to him! Bask in his love and ask him to remove every thread of selfishness from your heart. Write your prayer here:

2. Flip over to Philippians 2:1-4. Write down the unselfish things we're asked to do in these verses. How can you be a doer of these do's this week?

Random Acts of Love

Love is action! Here are a few ideas to get you started:

✿ Share your life with someone in need. Just pray and God will show you who.

✿ Organize a food drive for your local homeless shelter.

✿ Forgive your friends, even if they've really let you down.

✿ Go to a nursing home and give manicures.

✿ Send a card to or hug someone who is feeling down.

✿ Invite someone to church or youth group where they can hear the gospel.

✿ Pray for your family and friends. It's the coolest act of love!

✿ Put others' needs before your own.

✿ Love the Lord with all your heart, soul, and mind, and you will be full of loving actions!

As I have loved you, so you must love one another.

JOHN 13:34, NIV

Day Three

Jesus: The Ultimate Example

"Ah! You just wouldn't believe it," Deanna exclaimed when we arrived at Sunday school class.

"Believe what?" I asked.

"Karen!" she exclaimed, referring to her older sister. "She's in love. She used to be so mopey and boring, and now she's happy and giggly most of the time. It's like she glows."

I smiled.

"Last night she was practicing her ballet moves all over the house, like she was dancing on a cloud. I couldn't believe how she was acting!" Deanna sighed.

It's amazing how love changes a person! Knowing that someone cares about you and values you, gives a person a new sense of confidence. Karen was living proof. She developed a feeling of deep inner joy that showed up in her actions. All because of love!

The greatest example of life-changing love in the history of all humanity occurred nearly two thousand years ago. By a single selfless act, the meaning of love was forever changed.

John 15:13 tells us "Greater love has no one than this, that he lay down his life for his friends" (NIV).

That's exactly what Jesus did for us! He was willing to go to the cross and die an excruciating and shameful death. Why? To provide forgiveness for our sins and to bridge the gap between God and us. What was his motivation? Love!

Jesus loves us, and he proved it. In fact, Zechariah 2:8 says that we are the apple of his eye! And guess what? He's so crazy about you that he can't get you off his mind! Listen to this:

How precious it is, Lord, to realize that you are thinking about me constantly! I can't even count how many times a day your thoughts turn towards me. And when I waken in the morning, you are still thinking of me!

PSALM 139:17-18, TLB

Whoa!

When we realize how much Jesus has done for us and how very loved we are, it should bring us to our knees in gratitude. From there we can get up and let Jesus' example of love teach us how to love others.

After all, he's the expert on love. If he were taking Love 101, he'd get an A+. So, get out your Bible binoculars, 'cause we're going in for a closer look at exactly how he did it!

Jesus loved freely! Yep! No strings attached. That's called unconditional love. We didn't earn it and don't deserve it, but he loves us anyway. He wants us to love others as a free gift, too.

Jesus loved everyone! Yep! He told us to do the same—love our enemies, those who get under our skin, bug us, irritate us, and make us want to scream (see Matthew 5:43-47; Luke 6:35)!

God's love is really flowing through us when we reach out to the friendless who don't fit with the cool kids, those who are rude and do evil deeds. Hey—it's those who are toughest to love who need it the most!

Jesus' love was unending! Yep! He didn't give up on people. Peter, one of Jesus' twelve disciples, denied him three times, but Jesus didn't pull the love plug on Peter! With the Holy Spirit's help, we, too, can love those who have hurt us, ridiculed us, denied us, and lied about us.

Jesus' love was forgiving! Yep! He was beaten, rejected, cursed at, spit upon, mocked—you name it, he got it! But what did he say in those final moments of life? "Father, forgive them" (Luke 23:34, NIV). By an act of your will, you, too, can forgive those who mistreat you!

With the world's greatest example of love leading the way, you can have a forgiving, unending love that you can give away freely to everyone. You can love with Jesus' life-changing love!

Beauty Builders

1. Can anything separate us from God's glorious love? Find out in Romans 8:38-39. How does this make you feel?

2. Here are some orders straight from headquarters: *Love one another as I have loved you!* God's top priority is for us to love those he has placed in our lives, especially those in our families! List three ways you can do just that.

Day Four

She Let Go for Love

It was a dark day in the lives of God's people. The King of Egypt had just issued a proclamation that horrified every Hebrew mother! All male babies were to be killed at birth (see Exodus 1–2).

How awful! The Hebrew people worked as slaves in Egypt under the reign of Pharaoh, who noticed that no matter how hard he made them work, their population was increasing. He feared a potential takeover, so, to put a stop to their growing numbers, he ordered that all males born to the Hebrew women were to be thrown into the river to drown or to become dinner for the hungry crocodiles!

Upon hearing news of the Pharaoh's monstrous ruling, fear gripped the heart of Jochebed. She was pregnant! And she suspected the child growing within her was a boy.

A few months later her suspicions were confirmed! She gave birth to a beautiful baby boy. Jochebed instantly knew that this child was different, that God had a special mission for him. Her fear turned to faith! She couldn't let her baby be killed. As she snuggled the newborn close to her, she called out to Jehovah to help her hide her precious little one, her little one named Moses.

Keeping the baby quiet became a family project. Aaron and Miriam helped their parents keep Moses well-fed and entertained so he wouldn't cry and draw attention to his existence. How hard Miriam had to try not to slip up and tell her playmates about her adorable baby brother. It was the biggest secret ever!

When Moses was three months old, his mother knew she couldn't hide him much longer. Jochebed trusted God to show her how to keep this child alive, this child whom she deeply loved, this child whom God would use to deliver his people from the king of Egypt!

Early one morning, a plan was birthed in her heart! She gathered papyrus reeds and wove them into a basket. One morning, she fed little Moses, wrapped him in his favorite blanket, kissed his forehead, and set him in the basket.

Her heart pounded as she headed toward the river where she gently laid the basket among the reeds on the water's edge—safe from the crocodiles, safe from the Nile's strong currents, safe from the heat of the sun. Jochebed whispered a prayer of protection over her beloved son. Then she enlisted Miriam to stand guard, to see what would become of little Moses.

As God would have it, Pharaoh's daughter and her maids discovered Moses when they came to the river to bathe. The Pharaoh's daughter knew he was a Hebrew baby, but his bright eyes and chubby cheeks melted her heart, and she took the baby as her own.

Relief filled the heart of Jochebed. Her baby would live! Tears fell from her eyes. She would miss her little one, yet she was grateful to Jehovah for sparing his life.

What a courageous act! When Jochebed gave up Moses, whom she deeply loved, it was an incredible demonstration of the beautiful quality of love. Sometimes love demands such acts of selflessness. Sometimes love asks us to put others first and give up something we want. Yet, when we do, we allow love to blossom in our hearts. How beautiful!

Beauty Builders

1. Think back over the past few years of your life. What have you given up as an act of love? Perhaps you gave up music lessons when family funds were tight? Your spot in the band so a friend could have it? Your chance to go camping in order to stay home with your sick sibling? Or has someone given up something for you as an act of love?

2. What type of activities or relationships have you given up (or do you need to give up) because you love God?

Day Five

Getting Personal:
Looking at Your Love Life

A surefire way of knowing if someone is a Christian is by the love they have for others. Jesus said that if we love others the way he loves us, it will prove we are his disciples (see John 15:12-14).

Wow! Love is a big deal to God. So, it's time to get personal. It's time to take a look in your heart and find out where you are on the love scale!

Using the fifteen descriptions of love from 1 Corinthians 13:4-8, rate yourself in each area. Be honest. Be real. It's the only way to evaluate yourself effectively. Here we go!

1. Love is **PATIENT!** The line at the theater takes longer than normal. Do you:

5	4	3	2	1
remain calm		drop hints for others to hurry		demand action

2. Love is **KIND!** A classmate drops her books. Do you:

5	4	3	2	1
help pick them up		giggle		kick them further down the hall

3. Love is not **JEALOUS!** Your girlfriend got the part in the school play that you wanted. Are you:

5	4	3	2	1
genuinely happy		disappointed		green with envy

4. Love is not **PROUD!** You just won a beauty contest. Do you:

5	4	3	2	1
graciously say "Thanks"		gloat		wear your crown to school

5. Love is not **RUDE!** Your dog just nudged your elbow, sending your milkshake into the air. Do you:

5	4	3	2	1
laugh and let him lick it up		yell, then clean it up		smack him

6. Love is not **SELFISH!** You're in charge of prom decorations, but the chairperson just shared two ideas she likes better than yours. Would you:

5	4	3	2	1
be open to her ideas		refuse to listen		demand your way

7. Love is not easily **ANGERED!** Your sister has once again used your lip gloss without asking. Do you:

5	4	3	2	1
go buy her one of her own		talk to her politely		blow your top

8. Love does not hold **GRUDGES!** Your boyfriend refuses to attend your choir concert. Do you:

5	4	3	2	1
forgive him		give him the silent treatment		break it off

9. Love does not delight in **EVIL!** You just heard that a girl from your school had an abortion last week. Are you:

5	4	3	2	1
upset		a bit bothered		indifferent

10. Love rejoices with the **TRUTH!** All charges were dropped against your coach who was falsely accused of fraud. Do you:

5	4	3	2	1
write a note of support		help squelch rumors		do nothing

11. Love is **LOYAL!** You're so tired of listening to your friend complain. Do you:

5	4	3	2	1
quietly remain loyal	tell her enough's enough		ignore her phone calls

12. Love believes the **BEST!** You just caught your friend with her hands in your purse. She said that she just wanted to borrow your pen. Do you:

5	4	3	2	1
trust that she's truthful	question her motives		accuse her instantly

13. Love hopes for the **BEST!** Your older brother is running his first marathon. Before the race, do you:

5	4	3	2	1
plan a victory party	keep your fingers crossed		buy a sympathy card

14. Love **ENDURES!** You're splitting off from your family at the mall. Your little brother wants to come with you—again! Do you:

5	4	3	2	1
make him feel welcome	tolerate him		warn him to walk behind you

15. Love goes on **FOREVER!** Your dad promised to pitch you some balls this weekend and help you prepare for your big game, but he was too busy. Do you:

5	4	3	2	1
forgive him	say "It's OK"		tell everyone he doesn't really care

Tally up your points. Where are you on the Love Scale?

Scoring:

57–75 points: Way to go! The beautiful quality of love is shining through you. You are choosing to act and react in genuinely caring and selfless ways. Keep it up!

30–56 points: Not too bad! You are on the right track, but could use a little improvement. Ask yourself in each situation "How can I do the most loving thing in the most loving way?" Keep heading in the right direction!

20–29 points: Hmmm. Looks like you're struggling with love! Your first reaction might be selfish, sarcastic, rude, or impatient, but stop and think. Try not to let your actions be ruled by your feelings. Choose love. You can do it!

Below 20 points: Oh, boy! We need to talk ... and pray! You are definitely suffering from a love sickness! Is selfishness getting in the way of loving others? Have you offended others with your actions? Go to the Lord (and those you may have offended) and ask for forgiveness. Read God's Word during your daily quiet time. Ask God to fill you with his love.

Beauty Builders

1. In what type of situation is it hardest for you to be loving?

2. What could you do to become more loving?

3. Based on all you've learned this week about love, create a plan of action! Record it here:

Heavenly Father,
You demonstrate the beautiful quality of love to me over and over. You sent Jesus to die for my sins. You forgive me when I mess up. You are patient when I forget to pray. You are so good at loving me!
Father, your Word says that your love has been poured into my heart by the Holy Spirit. So, help me to grow in my capacity to express love for others so that I create a circle of love big enough for my family, friends, classmates, even my enemies to fit inside. Then I will be as loving as you are, and they will know that I love you and belong to you. In Jesus' name, Amen.

Weekend Journal

Write a letter to God expressing your gratitude for his love. Tell him what it means to you and what difference his love has made in your life.

Dear Heavenly Father,

With love,

_____

Chapter Three

Dazzlingly Delightful!

*The Beautiful Quality
of Joy*

You Mean Joy and Happiness Are Different?

"Joy is a deep sense of contentment, hope, and gratitude all bundled up together."
Zoe, 15

It had been a good day. No, a great day. Michelle had made it out of the house without a major blowup with her mom. She passed her Spanish quiz. And Brian had actually smiled at her when she cruised past him in the hall.

On top of all that, there was the tennis match. Thanks to her swift moves and powerful backhand, she blasted her opponent right off the court. Ah, the sweet taste of victory! She loved it. Michelle felt good. She felt powerful. She felt happy. Really happy.

Beth smiled as she laid her head back down on the pillow. Her room was filled with things she loved—ceramic angels, a Cubs poster, pictures of her family, notes from her friends, Scriptures taped to her dresser mirror. She was surrounded with reminders that despite her condition, she was loved. This gave her great joy.

The radiation and chemotherapy treatments had not been able to cure Beth's inoperable brain tumor. But even though she was physically weak, she was strong in spirit! She still loved to smother her baby sister with cuddles and kisses. She still enjoyed spending time making photo albums of her life. And she still treasured her long talks with her parents.

Most precious to Beth was her time with the Lord. She was so grateful to know that her life was right with God, that she was his child, that her sins had been forgiven, and that her destination was heaven. She was filled with a sense of gratitude and joy that caused her to rise above her current tragedy and enjoy her final days of life.

Michelle and Beth. Both of their stories are true (though the names have been changed to protect their identities). And on the surface, they both have smiles on their faces. But the reasons for those smiles are vastly different. See, Michelle's life is based on happiness. Beth's life is based on joy. The two are worlds apart!

Michelle was happy because things were going her way. Happiness is dependent upon what's happening around you, the behavior of others, and the events or circumstances surrounding your life. But life is fickle and people are undependable. There is no such thing as a perfect life!

What happens when Michelle fights with her mom, fails a test, loses a tennis match, and is totally ignored by Brian? Still happy? Nope. Happiness comes and goes based on life's circumstances. Life is full of upsets, disappointments, rejections, physical illnesses, crises, and stress … but you already knew that!

Happiness is not the beautiful quality that the Holy Spirit brings into our lives. He brings something much deeper, much longer lasting, much more fulfilling. He brings joy.

Joy is having a deep, ongoing, inner confidence in Christ that keeps you from being tossed back and forth by the winds of life. Joy is being hard-pressed on every side and still being able to trust God, no matter what.

Beth had discovered this secret key to joy. The smile on her face and the love that oozed from her being were proof that this beautiful quality of joy was hers, and no one could take that away from her!

Beauty Busters

1. Are you more like Michelle or Beth? Are you only happy when all is well, or is your pleasant disposition coming from something much deeper?

2. Your joy, or lack of it, usually shows up on your face and in your behavior. Read Proverbs 15:13 and 15:15. Jot down four ways you can visibly show joy!

1. _____ 3. _____

2. _____ 4. _____

3. Psalm 16:11 holds a fabulous truth. Read it then record some creative ways you can be in God's presence throughout each day.

Day Two

Battling the Blues

In a recent *USA Today* weekend survey, seven out of ten teens reported that they struggle with depression. Wow! That means there's a ton of teens feeling bummed! What's the deal?

There are many reasons why girls can feel blue: bad-hair days, flunking a driver's test, being overcommitted, wacky hormones, an unbalanced diet, just to name a few. Feeling down in the dumps every so often is perfectly normal. But with the Holy Spirit living inside of you, you don't have to stay there.

Depression, or feeling sad, is the opposite of being joyful. Allowing sadness and disappointment to linger in our lives zaps our ability to spread smiles, give words of encouragement, or reach out in love to others. Instead, we can become trapped in the pit of self-pity, bitterness, anger, and hopelessness. So, what's a girl to do when she's sitting in life's low-seat and battling the blues?

Take whatever has you feeling down and lift it up to the Lord! Trust the fact that God is completely trustworthy. He can handle what's got you down. He can be the source of your joy. Let's look at each of these a little more closely!

First, God is totally trustworthy. When life's not going the way you want it to go, you can count on the fact that ultimately God is in control. Therefore, you can trust him. He takes all the broken pieces of your life and melds them together to create something beautiful (my personal paraphrase of Romans 8:28). That's God's job! Your job is to give your expectations of life over to him.

When you expect life to go to the right, but it takes a major detour to the left, it won't throw you so far off course if you let go of expectations and trust God with your life.

When I was modeling in New York City, I had a major encounter with God. I knew he wanted me to leave the city—and my career—and go back home to follow *his* plan for my life! It wasn't what I had expected! At first, I allowed it to get me down. After all, I would be giving up my lifelong dream.

But as I sent up my spiritual antenna, I began to see what God had planned for me. I gave up my expectations and let *him* call the shots! To this day, I know I can count on him to take care of whatever happens in my life. He is trustworthy!

Second, God is the source of our joy. We have reason to rejoice every minute, every second! As Christians, we have forgiveness of sins. Our sins are gone—outta here! That's a wonderfully good thing. We have eternal life—we're not headed for the hot spot—we are heaven-bound! Yes! We can rejoice in the fact that God is who he says he is and that he loves us. No matter how we feel, these facts are true, and we can give thanks for them every day!

But there's a little catch here. You and I must *choose* to be joyful. We must choose to be thankful! First Thessalonians 5:18 tells us to give thanks *in* all things! It does not say give thanks *for* all things.

For example, when I left New York, my friends made fun of me and accused me of failing. I was not thankful *for* the situation, but I chose to be thankful *in* the situation. I chose to praise God and be joyful that he was at work in my life (whether my friends understood it or not).

God is the source of my joy. Is he yours? If you look around, you will see that God has placed bundles of blessings and little jots of joy all around you. Being joyful is like a strong medicine that will take your heavy heart and make it merry!

My dear friend, God is the source of my joy—and of yours. But sometimes we need help to see that. If you are battling an ongoing feeling of sadness, you may be seriously depressed and in need of professional help. Clinical depression is not a sign of weakness or a character flaw. It results from a chemical imbalance in the body. The good news is that depression can be successfully treated.

Open up to your parents, a trusted teacher, a school counselor, a friend's mom, or your youth pastor, someone who can help you get what you need to blast that depression right out of your heart! Plus, here are a few organizations that may be of help: Rapha (a Christian organization), Covenant House, and Youth Crisis Hotline. Their toll-free numbers may be obtained by calling directory assistance for 800 numbers (800-555-1212).

Beauty Builders

1. Are you struggling with depression, sadness, or disappointment? Go ahead and tell God about it right here. Then read Nehemiah 8:10.

2. What expectations are you holding on to that need to be given over to God? Write a prayer of relinquishment here.

Day Three

Jesus: Energized by Joy

Sunny days and sunblock! Lips and lipstick! Mousse and mega hair! Working out and sweat! Bookmarks and books! Here's another pair of words that go together: Jesus and Joy.

Joy played a big-time role in Jesus' life. Joy was his motivator. Joy was his fuel. Joy was his energizer!

Check this out:

> *He was willing to die a shameful death on the cross because of the JOY he knew would be his afterwards; and now he sits in the place of honor by the throne of God.*
>
> HEBREWS 12:2, TLB

Jesus endured a shameful death on the cross. It was shameful because he was falsely accused of blasphemy against God. Shameful because it was the way criminals died. He also suffered a death that was painful—both physically and emotionally. Physically he was spit upon, was beaten, had his beard pulled out, was nailed to the cross, and was crucified. Emotionally he was betrayed, rejected, mocked, and denied.

Yet, joy got him through! It was for the joy that was before him that he was able to endure the cross.

What could possibly bring so much joy to Jesus' heart that he was willing to go through the crucifixion experience?

You.

Me.

Jesus knew that if he died on the cross, he would wipe out our sin debt. He would make a way for us to be made clean and holy. It would then be possible for us to have a relationship with God the Father.

He also knew that his Father would raise him from the dead, thus defeating death and Satan.

He knew that heaven's doors would be opened, and we could have eternal life. You and I, forever in the presence of God!

Jesus also knew he would be reunited with his Father. Yep! When all was said and done, he would return to his heavenly home and sit down on the throne at the place of honor—right beside his Dad.

Each of these things brought him an incredible and glorious joy.

Each of these things propelled him to push through the pain, hardship, and public humiliation.

The beautiful quality of joy helped Jesus to:

1. *Fix his eyes on the final outcome.*

2. *Trust God to pull him through.*

3. *Put up with the rejection and mockery of others (who didn't understand God's plan).*

4. *Endure tough circumstances and situations that he didn't choose, but that God asked him to walk through.*

Can we learn from Jesus' example? Absolutely!

No matter what kinds of problems try to steal our joy, we can trust God to pull us through. We can let go of the teasing from others, knowing that God is on our side. And we can be confident that when all is said and done, we will see him face to face!

That, girlfriend, will be ultimate joy!

Beauty Builders

1. Jesus let joy be his motivating force. Then he was rewarded (seated next to God in heaven) and got even more joy! Think of a time when you were obedient, and God rewarded you with joy. Share it here:

2. When you are being teased, mocked, or rejected by others, how can fixing your eyes on Christ and trusting God pull you through?

Random Acts of Joy

You can do a lot more than just jump for joy. Check out this jazzy joy list. You can put a smile on your face and someone else's, today!

✿ Tell someone about Christ.

✿ Smile at a stranger while you're sitting in traffic.

✿ Take a friend out to lunch.

✿ Look through family photo albums.

✿ Worship the Lord! It will absolutely lighten your heart.

✿ Take a bubble bath.

✿ Write someone a thank-you letter.

✿ Tell the truth!

✿ Get outside—feed some ducks, pick a flower.

✿ Learn to laugh at yourself.

✿ Every time you get blessed, write it down and put it in a special jar. Then when you need to be encouraged, pull a blessing out to read.

"...obey my commands ... so that my joy may be in you and that your joy may be complete."

JOHN 15:10, 11 NIV

Day Four

And Mary Rejoiced!

Mary sat on an old wooden stool, wiping the dust from her sandal-clad feet. She didn't have much time to spare. It was nearly time to help her mother prepare the evening meal. She didn't mind kneading the bread or stirring the pot of simmering vegetables.

Mary was an ordinary girl who called Nazareth home. She had always believed in God, enjoyed morning prayers and Sabbath days at the temple. But never, in her wildest dreams, could she have imagined the plan God had for her life.

Oh, she knew she was going to marry Joseph, the fine, upstanding, honest carpenter who had won her heart. But to become the mother of the Messiah? Whoa! That was certainly not what she had expected!

But it was true. The angel had said so! Mary had found favor with God, and he had chosen to bless her with the honor of bearing his Son!

Yes, of course, she was confused! She was a virgin! How could she have a baby?

But this was one informed angel! He had all the answers. He told her:

> *The Holy Spirit shall come upon you, and the power of God shall overshadow you; so the baby born to you will be utterly holy—the Son of God.*
>
> LUKE 1:35, TLB

With great excitement, mixed with humility and honor, Mary accepted her assignment.

I am the Lord's servant, and I am willing to do whatever he wants. May everything you said come true.

LUKE 1:38, TLB

Because the angel had also informed her that her cousin Elizabeth, who was once barren, was also pregnant, Mary packed up and went to visit her.

"Cousin Elizabeth, are you here? It's Mary." At the sound of Mary's greeting, Elizabeth's baby (John the Baptist) jiggled around inside his mother's womb with joy! Mary and Elizabeth clasped hands and danced around the kitchen, laughing and crying at the incredible miracles God was performing in their lives.

Mary's voice was passionate as she exclaimed:

Oh, how I praise the Lord. How I rejoice in God my Savior! For he took notice of his lowly servant girl, and now generation after generation forever shall call me blest of God.

LUKE 1:46-48, TLB

Mary's character was revealed by her response to the unexpected in her life. God had called her to do something she had not planned on doing. How did she react?

She rejoiced!

That's how you can tell if a person has the beautiful quality of joy in their life. They rejoice!

Rejoice is an action word. It means to speak of the blessing of God. To be filled with delight! To overflow with joy—allowing it to splash over onto others.

Mary rejoiced in God because of what he was doing in her life. She was glad he had chosen her—an ordinary girl for an extraordinary task! She beamed with joy and glowed with gratitude.

Rejoicing makes you attractive inside and out. People will be drawn to your pleasant disposition, your happy attitude, and your friendly nature. Have you ever seen a smiling face that was *not* beautiful? Smiles are inviting! They are a sign of a heart that is cheerful.

Rejoice and praise God for what he is doing in your life, whether you expected it or not, whether you like it or not. Rejoicing will fill your heart with joy and cause you to be dazzlingly delightful!

Beauty Builders

1. If God showed up right now, right where you are, and he rearranged your entire life (like he did Mary's), would you respond with joy? Why or why not?

2. Philippians 4:4 tells us to always rejoice! Rejoicing is especially important when you don't feel like it. But feelings can be affected by actions. Rejoice first, then the right feelings will follow. Are you struggling with an unpleasant situation right now? Ask the Holy Spirit to fill you with joy, and then begin to speak words of rejoicing. Write your prayer here.

Day Five

Getting Personal:
Are You Building or Blasting Joy?

Karen admitted to me that she struggles with joy. She has a hard time seeing the positive side of things. Clearly, this was obvious to others, because her grandfather teased her a lot.

He recently said, "Karen, honey, let's say there was half a glass of juice setting on the table. Is that glass half full or half empty?"

Karen laughed. "I said it was half empty, which caused Granddad to laugh, because he knew I was going to say that. He lovingly smiled and went on to explain that an optimist—a girl who looks for the good in life—would say it was half full. But a pessimist (yep, the girl who tends to only see the negative) would say it was half empty. Guess I'm a pessimist, but I'm working on switching sides!"

Like Karen, are you struggling with your choice to rejoice?

Let's find out! It's time to figure out if you are building or blasting joy in your life.

When the squeeze is on, which of these words best describes what squirts out of you? Read the first line, then check the one that applies. Be honest!

Joy Builders	**Joy Blasters**
☐ contentment	☐ complaining
☐ gratefulness	☐ grumpiness
☐ generosity	☐ selfishness
☐ forgiveness	☐ resentment

Joy Builders

- ☐ encouragement
- ☐ excitement
- ☐ delight
- ☐ peace
- ☐ flexibility
- ☐ calmness
- ☐ God-focus
- ☐ confidence
- ☐ friendliness

Joy Blasters

- ☐ discouragement
- ☐ apathy
- ☐ depression
- ☐ argument
- ☐ perfectionism
- ☐ anger
- ☐ self-focus
- ☐ self-consciousness
- ☐ unfriendliness

Count up the number of checks in each column. How did you do? Are you building joy or blasting it right out of your life?

Remember, you are not alone! The Holy Spirit is right there to fill you with joy and to shine through you.

Late at night, what do you see when you look up into the sky? The moon! But how can you see the moon? It has no light of its own!

Ah, but it does reflect light. That's right. The sun shines into the surface of the moon, which reflects those sunny rays!

Sometimes, we don't have joy of our own, do we? We need to turn and face the Lord and allow his joy to shine on us so that we can reflect it to others.

Remember, we need to stay connected to the Vine in order to be filled with joy. And when we do, our beauty is boundless. We are definitely dazzlingly delightful!

Beauty Builders

1. What are you facing right now that is zapping your joy?

2. Review your list of Joy Blasters. What changes do you need to make in your attitudes, your habits, or your life to become a more joyful person?

3. Based on all you've learned this week about joy, create a plan of action.

Heavenly Father,
Help me to see you as the source of my joy. Help me to see where you are at work in my life, and cause me to be more trusting of your special plan for me.

Give me, Father, the courage to give thanks in all things and to realize the choice to rejoice is mine.

Above all, fill me with the Holy Spirit's joy, and remind me that my joy is not based on changeable circumstances but on my relationship with you and the eternal life you have promised me. In Jesus' name, Amen.

Weekend Journal

Write a letter to the Lord thanking him for all the things, events, and people in your life that bring you joy. Then let those joys fill up your heart and give praise to the Lord. Sing him a song of praise, applaud him, dance before him! Not only will you be filled with joy, but so will he!

Dear Heavenly Father,

With love,

_____

Chapter Four

Captivatingly Calm!

*The Beautiful Quality
of Peace*

Living In Harmony

"Peace is not being trouble-free or in an altered state of consciousness! It's having a calm, inner sense of confidence that comes from your connection to God!"
Lisa, 16

L eave me alone!" Kim screamed at her dad. Wham! Her bedroom door slammed shut. She threw herself on her bed. How could her dad expect her to be excited about his promotion? Moving five hundred miles away did not exactly fit into her plan for her junior year. She had just been elected class secretary! And what about her job at the vet's clinic? She loved helping to care for the animals.

Then there were Krysta and Beccie. It would kill her to leave her two best friends in the whole world. No, she was far from excited. She was scared and angry and upset. Moving meant she would be alone in a new school, in a new city.

Kim winced as the knot in her stomach tightened. She turned on her CDs to drown out the thoughts racing through her mind. But what she really needed was a huge portion of peace.

There are a bazillion different ways to describe peace. I would like to define it as living in harmony with others.

Kim was struggling with this. In one sixty-second encounter, she had stirred up a storm of conflict between herself and her dad!

Is it possible to live in harmony with family and friends? Yep!

In fact, God calls us to be peacemakers. He wants us to be mix-up menders, conflict crushers, quarrel quenchers! Especially when it comes to our relationships with those two VIPs he has placed in our lives: OUR PARENTS!

He wants us to choose to communicate instead of thinking rotten thoughts or harboring feelings that will come crashing down at some point. We must refuse to yell, fight, or issue the silent treatment. We need to learn to talk it out and negotiate. Whether the issue is over curfew, CDs, chores, or classes, it's time to call a truce and come to a compromise!

Tips to help you deal with parents

1. *Pray!* Never attempt to resolve conflict without prayer.
2. *Respect* your parents' God-given role. They are responsible for you and are there to protect you. "No" is sometimes the most loving answer they can give you.
3. *Cool off!* Get rid of emotion before you try to talk things out. Anger only fuels conflict. As Proverbs 15:1 says, "A gentle answer turns away wrath" (NIV).
4. *Write it out!* Put your thoughts and feelings down on paper. Write out your goal—how you want the conflict to be resolved. Now reread it. Once it's out of you, you may see the situation differently.
5. *Remember your parents' personalities are different from yours.* They will have a different perspective. Sometimes there is not a right or wrong perspective, just different. That is why communication is so important.
6. *As you come together, try to pray as a family.* Then ask lots of questions in an effort to gather facts and understand

where your parents are coming from. If you don't understand something, ask them to clarify it. Or say "What I
think you are saying is ... Is this correct?" Then let them
respond. Don't ask accusatory questions like "Why don't
you trust me?" or "Why are you so old-fashioned?"

7. *Watch your words!* Think before you speak. Don't blame.
Own your statements, saying, "I feel that ..." instead of
"You made me feel...." Avoid words like *never*, *always*,
and *every time*. They lead to exaggerations.

8. *Accept their final decision.* God wants you to honor and
respect your parents, to treat them like VIPs! Resolving
conflict is really not about winning. It's about better
understanding, clearer communication, and coming to a
place of peace. Peace may not come until you yield your
will. You will not only please your earthly parents, but
you'll please your heavenly one, too.

Beauty Builders

1. Are you currently in conflict with your parents? Tell God about
it in the space below and ask him to give you the courage to talk it
out with them.

2. God has given your parents a responsibility. Read about it in
Proverbs 22:6. Read about your responsibility in Ephesians 6:1-3.
What could you do to help make your parents' job easier, and
thereby have more peace at home?

Day Two

What's Up With Worry?

Have you ever felt like a *Hystrix africaeaustralis*? Well, I have! That's just the official name for a crested porcupine! Whenever this creature feels threatened, worried, unprotected, or overly sensitive, he raises his quills to protect himself. He goes for that bristled look!

We tend to react the same way when we're struggling with anger, frustration at school, time pressures, overcommitment, term papers, and band tryouts. Unless, of course, we have peace. Then our quills are down, our look is sleek. Ooh! How captivatingly calm! What a sweet fashion statement!

Peace looks good on you. But not just any peace. God's peace! How do we get it? Glad you asked! Listen to this:

> *Don't worry about anything; instead, pray about everything; tell God your needs and don't forget to thank him for his answers. If you do this you will experience God's peace, which is far more wonderful than the human mind can understand. His peace will keep your thoughts and your hearts quiet and at rest as you trust in Christ Jesus.*
>
> PHILIPPIANS 4:6-7, TLB

Let's examine this passage from Philippians bit by bit to get a better understanding of how this works.

Instead of worrying, we are to trust the Lord and pray about everything. Tell all your needs to God. He wants you to talk to him about every trouble, every problem, every worry, every stress. He is interested in every detail of your life. Don't hold back; let him have it all!

Whenever possible, choose a quiet place for prayer. When there's lots of distraction, we can forget what we're trying to say. The Bible says Jesus usually went to the mountains to be alone and pray. It was quiet and he could openly pour out his heart to his Father God.

Well, we don't have to go the mountains. The idea is to find a quiet place. Matthew 6:6 says to go away by yourself and close the door. Then with openness, honesty, and boldness pray to the Lord.

Of course, we can't always have it completely quiet. Many times during the hustle and busyness of the day we need to shoot those quickie prayers up to God. Yet, for your longer prayer times, quiet and solitude are helpful.

Keep a prayer journal handy. Use a booklet with blank pages or a spiral notebook. Write down the date, your prayer requests, and then leave a space to write in the answers and the dates the answers were given. It helps to look back and see how God has worked in your life. It also reminds you that God does, indeed, answer prayer.

Our next instruction is to thank God for his answers, even before they come. After you have told God your needs, right away start thanking him for the solutions and answers! Why thank God before he has done anything? Two reasons.

First, thanking him ahead of time shows him you have faith that he will, indeed, give you an answer. Second, it makes you expect an answer! Often, we say a little prayer, walk away, and forget we even prayed at all. Later, we can't remember if God ever did anything.

Our part is to pray. God's part is to answer. So thank him right away and expectantly wait for him to respond.

If you stop worrying, pray about everything, tell God your needs, and thank him for his answers, what do you get? God's peace! God exchanges your prayer needs, your worries, your fears, your stresses for his peace. What a deal!

Better yet, it is a peace that is so wonderful, your mind can't understand it. Here you have all these troubles and you should be completely stressed, but you're not. You're peaceful. Calm. Confident. You're amazed at your response, and so are others.

God's peace has a way of keeping your heart and mind quiet and restful. When you entrust your needs to Jesus, his peace will be yours.

Beauty Builders

1. My husband always says that trust and worry can't be "on the swing" in our hearts at the same time! Which one seems to be on your swing these days? Why?

2. There's a great promise in Isaiah that you'll love! Read it in chapter 26, verse 3! What is the promise? List three ways you can keep your thoughts on Christ so his peace will fill your heart.

1. _____

2. _____

3. _____

Random Acts of Peace

Here are some positively posh thoughts on how to bring more peace into your whirlwind world!

❁ Pray! Pray! Pray!

❁ Obey your parents.

❁ Mend broken relationships!

❁ Don't let the sun go down on your anger.

❁ Get a daily planner and keep track of life.

❁ Dig into God's Word!

❁ Learn to accept yourself. Don't compare yourself with others!

❁ Forget about trying to blend God's ways and the world's ways.

❁ Let go of fear, take hold of faith.

❁ Take a private walk-and-talk with God.

❁ Meditate on the fact that God is all-knowing, totally powerful, and ever-present.

❁ Be quick to say, "I'm sorry."

❁ Do your best; let God do the rest.

❁ Do something nice for someone who upset you.

Happy are those who strive for peace—they shall be called the sons of God.

MATTHEW 5:9, TLB

Day Three

Jesus: Snoozin' and Cruisin'

Jesus and the boys didn't seem to notice the change in weather as they got into the boat and headed across the lake. It had been several long days of ministry, teaching the great crowd about the kingdom of God, praying for the needs of many, and feeding thousands from only a couple of fish and one loaf of bread!

Jesus was tired. He went to the back of the boat, laid down on a cushion, and crashed! Asleep in seconds! He rested knowing that much had been accomplished.

The rest of the passengers, however, were not so peaceful. The storm had come up quickly. The darkened, moisture-filled clouds had finally let loose, and it was pouring down rain. The wind had emerged with great force.

Peter and John watched intently. The concern in the former fishermen's eyes turned to fear. The waves were crashing up over the sides of the boat, filling it with salty seawater. The boat was being tossed from side to side as the gusts of wind caught the sails. Surely they would not survive this. Surely they were going to drown.

Searching the deck, Peter and John didn't see Jesus anywhere. Where was he? Ah, he had gone to take a snooze! They went to find him, assuming he would have been jolted out of his beauty sleep. But no. There he was, resting comfortably.

They shook him into consciousness. "Master, Master, we are sinking," they cried. In other words, "What are you doing? We are all going to die here! It's *hasta la vista* for you, us, and the rest of the boys! Don't you care? Wake up! We're about to go under!"

Jesus made his way to the front of the boat, not to pick up a bucket and start bailing water, but to show the disciples, once again, exactly who he was.

He stood strong, faced the storm, and said, "Peace, be still." And it was! The wind and the waves obeyed. The rain stopped. All was calm!

Jesus turned to the disciples. "Where is your faith?" he asked.

Their mouths dropped open. Some were scratching their heads. Others were catching their breath. "Did you see that? Even the wind and waves obey him." They shivered in awe.

But why were they so shocked? They had seen Jesus heal people. They had seen him feed thousands with so little food. Yet, they panicked in the storm! Why? Because they saw the wind, the waves, and the water in the boat, and forgot that the very Son of God, the Prince of Peace himself, was right there with them in the middle of it all. (Read the story in Matthew 8:23-27 and Luke 8:22-25.)

We, too, will face storms in this life. The storm could be the divorce of your parents, the death of a grandparent, a friend on drugs, a secret sin, an unexpected illness. But remember: Take your eyes off of the storm and run to Jesus! He is right there with you. He is your peace. Jesus says that his peace is not like the world's peace.

Peace I leave with you; My peace I give to you; not as the world gives, do I give to you.

JOHN 14:27, NASB

The world's idea of peace is having a smooth-sailing, trouble-free life. Well sure, if you move to the top of a mountain or to the deserted desert where there is no one around to bother you, it will be peaceful. But Jesus knows that is not very realistic, nor is that what he wants for our lives.

He has asked us to be lights in our world, to get involved, and show others who he is. The Lord knows our lives will be stormy at times, and so he offers a different kind of peace. Not peace on the outside, but peace on the inside.

In your times of trouble, when the winds of life are blowing and the waves are crashing against you, listen very carefully and you will hear, "Peace, be still. I am here. You are not going to drown. You and I together will weather this storm." Those are words you can count on!

Beauty Builders

1. What storms are you facing right now in your life? Bring Jesus into the middle of them. Read Psalm 46:10. How can realizing that God is God make a difference in your storms?

2. Sometimes Jesus calms our storms; sometimes he calms us in the midst of the storms! Either way, he makes us a promise. Read Psalm 23:4 and Hebrews 13:5. What is that promise? Write a prayer thanking God for being a promise-keeper!

Day Four

Martha:
Portrait of a Whirlwind Woman

Serene. Peaceful. Quiet. Calm. Tranquil. Composed. These are not words that would best describe Martha, the sister of Lazarus and Mary. She was one of Jesus' closest friends. But easygoing? No way!

Martha knew Jesus was in town, so she invited him over for a big spaghetti dinner. (OK, maybe it wasn't spaghetti, but I get to tell the story my way!)

Martha welcomed her guests with a big smile and a warm hug. She ushered them into the living room where they could relax and chat while she headed for the kitchen and sprang into action. Pots and pans clanked. The sound of cutting and chopping filled the kitchen. The meat was frying, the water was boiling, and the sauce was simmering. But she still needed to blend the oil and vinegar for the salad dressing, prepare the garlic bread, and stir up the brownies for dessert.

The kitchen looked like a three-ring circus. The counter was splattered with spaghetti sauce. The noodles were boiling over. The garlic bread was burning up, and so was Martha! In fact, she was fuming! Why wasn't Mary helping her? Was she expected to make dinner single-handedly? She had wanted to serve such a special meal for Jesus, but it was about to blow up in her face!

Instead, Martha blew up! She marched into the living room and exploded! With hands on her hips, she got in Jesus' face. "Lord, what's the deal? This is not fair! I'm working like crazy and Mary's just sitting here listening to you! Tell her to get into the kitchen and help me!" (Ha! For the real quote see Luke 10:40.)

With gentleness and patience, Jesus responded, "Martha, dear friend, you are so upset over all these details! There is really only one thing worth being concerned about. Mary has discovered it—and I won't take it away from her!" (Luke 10:41-42, TLB).

Martha was busy, distracted, upset, bossy, impatient, and wound a little too tight!

Mary was calm and content, sitting at Jesus' feet, listening to his teachings and enjoying his presence.

Martha was serving the Lord, which was great, but she lost sight of what was truly important. She was focused on physical food, while Mary was focused on spiritual food.

Jesus said that Mary had chosen the "good part, the one thing to be concerned about." What was it? Him! Sitting at his feet, feeding on his words, nourishing her soul with his abiding presence. That was Mary's priority!

Are you more like Martha or Mary? When you've got chores to do, do you:

a. Get upset and share your crabby mood with others?
b. Work at the speed of light, trying to get it all done while your heart pounds in your chest because you're totally stressed?
c. Go to the Lord, pray over each demand of the day and ask him to give you peace?
d. Ask God to help you clearly see which things are most important to him and then do those first?

If you answered A or B, you're a Martha kind of gal! If C or D best describe you, you're more the Mary type!

Being too busy and overinvolved can rob you of inner peace. Distractions, deadlines, and duties can pull you away from the

Lord. There are lots of good things to be involved in, but if you're hammered with headaches, you can't sleep, you trample on anyone who gets in your way, or you recoil in fear of failing to follow through on all your commitments, then it is not worth it! It is *not* good. You'll have no peace, no joy, no life. And chances are, you'll have squeezed Jesus right out of your schedule!

Take some time today to think about your church activities, your classes, your homework load, your part-time job, and your sports, drama, or musical involvement. Then tomorrow you'll be ready to do some serious business with God.

Beauty Builders

1. Martha and Mary both loved Jesus, but they behaved differently. How are you like Martha? Like Mary? Why?

2. Jesus was never in a hurry; he was never late for an appointment! Read Luke 5:15-16. There were crowds waiting to hear and see Jesus. He let them wait. There was something he wanted to go do. What was it? Just like Jesus, how can you keep the main thing (God) the main thing?

Day Five

Getting Personal:
Are You Keeping First Things First?

Today's teens (that's you!) live very full lives. Think about it! There's school, sports, family, friends, jobs, play practice, youth group, church. Not to mention the daily hassle of figuring out what to wear and how to fix your hair!

Does trying to juggle everything give you the jitters? Does the balancing act put a pinch in your peace? Well, take off your headset, turn off the TV, push aside your homework, and turn on your answering machine, because it's time to get quiet before God! It's time to see if there are things in your life that are robbing you of inner peace.

Let's prioritize! In column A, from one to twelve, rank the following things in order of most to least important, with number one getting top billing. Then, in column B, cruise back down the list and rank them according to time. Which things take up most of your time? Which take least? Remember, everything can't be a top priority.

A   B

____ ____   Going to class and doing homework

____ ____   Attending youth group/Bible study, church

____ ____   Working a part-time job

____ ____   Being involved with drama, music, or sports

____ ____   Having a daily quiet time to pray, confess, and read the Bible

A B

___ ___ Taking private lessons (musical instrument, acting, academics)

___ ___ Having dinner with family or family activity nights

___ ___ Working out/keeping fit

___ ___ Volunteering (Christian service)

___ ___ Hanging out with friends

___ ___ Watching TV, listening to music, surfing the net

___ ___ Looking good—hair, nails, clothes

___ ___ Other: _____

Finished? OK! Here's the big question: Are the things you listed as most important the same things that are occupying most of your time? Are you giving an appropriate amount of attention to the things that really matter?

Which items on the list are distracting you from the valuable, meaningful activities of life?

Which items are crowding out your quiet time with God?

If you didn't have to be concerned about living up to someone else's expectations or about grades or money or your social reputation, what changes would you make in your life? Which activities on your list would you like to (or need to) let go of?

Review these last few pages. Do you see any patterns? Is the Holy Spirit trying to tell you something? Are there changes you need to make so that you can have more peace in your life? Record them here:

This was a tough challenge today, but hopefully you found it insightful. Make the changes you can. Be aware of anything that steals your time with the Lord and squeezes the peace right out of your life.

Beauty Builders

1. What things in your life are robbing you of God's peace or tempting you to be anxious and worried?

2. How could having more peace add to the quality of your life?

3. Based on everything you've learned this week, create a plan of action.

Heavenly Father,
I now understand that if I resolve conflict in my relation-ships, if I refuse to let distractions steal my time with you, and that if I bring you right into the midst of my storms, I will have peace.
Father, help me to set aside worry, to lay my needs at your feet, and to remember you are only a whisper away. Thank you from the bottom of my peaceful heart! In Jesus' name, Amen.

Weekend Journal

Write a letter to God expressing your desire to keep him at the very center of your life. Tell him what that means to you, and share from your heart the things you need to change in order to put him there. Close your prayer by thanking him for bringing his peace into your life.

Dear Heavenly Father,

With love,

_____

Chapter Five

Elegantly Even-Tempered!

*The Beautiful Quality
of Patience*

When the Pressure Is On

*"Patience is the ability to stay joyful and
peaceful while driving behind a car going
25 mph when the speed limit is 55 mph
and you are late."*
Erin, 18

I've watched her for the last several years. Sometimes up close, sometimes from a distance. When her Sunday school class is not paying attention, she rings her bell, then stands quietly with a smile on her face. I have never heard her raise her voice.

When she heard that her friend's son was on drugs, she didn't tell everyone the new, juicy gossip. Instead, she challenged each of us to pray for the young man.

When her mother was ill for a long time, she didn't complain, she just kept caring for her as needed. When serving with her on a committee, I've heard her share her opinion, but she never demands her own way.

This godly woman has been an excellent example for me. She has been the perfect picture of the beautiful quality of patience.

My own picture is not quite so pretty. When my senior high Sunday school class is ignoring me and carrying on their own private conversations while I'm trying to teach, I yell into the microphone and tell them to pipe down! (That may sound extreme, but hey, there are sixty-five of them and only one of me!)

When I catch wind of some gossip, it kills me to keep my mouth shut! And ailments? Who's got time to pamper someone else? I always have something of my own that hurts!

I confess! I'm an impatient complainer! God and I have a ways to go in the area of patience.

Exactly what is patience? Let's listen in and see how these gorgeous gals define this very *chic* quality.

Chick Chat

Hurry! Give me your definition of patience!

Patience is waiting without complaining, knowing that the waiting time will be used by God for your good. God will answer eventually!

Jen, 16

Patience is the ability to remain good-natured and positive under pressure.

Frances, 14

Patience is like a sweet honey that draws others to us and helps us to be compatible.

Wendy, 14

Patience is a vital component in our everyday lives. In fact, in the New Testament, most of the verses on patience refer to our relationships with others. It doesn't speak so much of being patient with things (like a car that won't start) or with events (longer-than-life lines at the drive-through). Instead, the Scriptures make the point that patience is a prime part of our dealings with a nagging mom, a little brother who trashes the bathroom, the girl that sits behind you in class and constantly clicks her nails, or the friend that continually leaks your personal business to the entire cheerleading squad!

Got people? Get patience!

God calls us to be patient people. It is an expression of love (see 1 Corinthians 13:4). It keeps us from losing our temper when someone makes us angry. It helps us to hang in there with a friend who never fails to do things we just don't understand. It calms us when we're tempted to push our personal agenda. It allows us to maintain control of our tongues when we've been insulted or embarrassed.

It is a true expression of Christlike character—waiting in line, remaining quiet when we are inconvenienced, letting others go first, and not demanding our own way.

Perhaps you've already made this big discovery, but when you pray for patience, you can count on God to send you people and circumstances that give you the opportunities to practice being patient! When you turn to him for help, he will spot you as you pump up those patience muscles. Welcome those opportunities. They are building a beautiful you.

Beauty Builders

1. Patience can become a natural result of abiding in the Vine, but it is also a choice that we make—usually a split-second decision! How do you think choosing to be patient with people can improve your relationships?

2. Are you a patient person? Why or why not? How could you become more patient?

Day Two

An Award-Winning Performance? Not!

Pretending to be patient is not the same as the real thing. Tolerance is not the real thing. Putting up with a person who is making your skin crawl is not the real thing. Biting your tongue while plotting revenge is not the real thing.

Apathy is a counterfeit, too. Appearing to be patient when really you don't give a rip is not the same as true godly patience. Apathy plays out as indifference. Patience plays out as intentional restraint—holding back and maintaining composure because you care!

Real patience is not just playing a part in a performance or acting out a scene like a skillful actress. True patience responds very differently from its popular impostors. When the pressure's on, what would patience do? How does the real thing respond? Let's find out!

True patience responds ...

With Prayer! Immediately go to God and ask the Holy Spirit to fill you with his patience! Will he do it? Yep. "This is the confidence we have in approaching God: that if we ask anything according to his will, he hears us. And if we know that he hears us—whatever we ask—we know that we have what we asked of him" (1 John 5:14-15, NIV). Being patient is definitely his will. So, ask and you shall receive!

With Forgiveness! When you've been hurt, true patience chooses not to hold a grudge. Patience allows hurts to melt away and continues to offer love and acceptance. Jesus tells us to forgive over and over! Peter asks Jesus if we should forgive seven times. Jesus said, "No, seventy times seven!" (See Matthew 18:22.) Did he mean exactly 490 times and no more? Nope. He was making a point. The point—always forgive!

With Righteous Acts! True patience chooses not to allow another person's actions to dictate our reactions and cause us to sin! Ephesians 4:26-27 gives us guidelines to live by: "Be angry, and yet do not sin; do not let the sun go down on your anger, and do not give the devil an opportunity" (NASB). Satan would love for you to toss patience out the door and lose your temper. Don't do it! Don't let the devil win!

With Mercy! "Give them what they deserve! They've got it coming!" Is that what true patience would say? Nada! Patience responds with mercy. Mercy is not giving others what they deserve. You're not responsible for paybacks. That's God's job. He says "Vengeance is Mine, I will repay" (Hebrews 10:30, NASB). So don't get angry or make threats. Choose to be kind and merciful.

With Blessing! That's right. No tongue-lashings allowed! True patience blesses others—even when they've said something rotten. First Peter 3:8-9 proves it, saying, "To sum up, let all be harmonious, sympathetic, brotherly, kindhearted, and humble in spirit; not returning evil for evil, or insult for insult, but giving a blessing instead" (NASB).

When you struggle to be patient and to maintain your composure, just remember: Don't fake it, faith it! Call on the Holy One! He will help you to be elegantly even-tempered.

Beauty Builders

1. Think of a time when someone offended you or insulted you and you responded with patient mercy. Now think of an incident where you reacted in rage or revenge. What was the final outcome of each situation?

2. True patience or longsuffering means to keep on keeping on, even when there is pressure! Are you in now or have you recently been in a situation that was unpleasant but required you to hang tough? Write a short prayer asking God to help you to be patient.

Day Three

The King of Patience

The kingdom of heaven can be compared to a king (we'll call him King Justly) whose huge dynasty had fallen behind in the billing department. He sent a memo ordering all accounts to be brought up to date.

In the process, King Justly learned that one man (we'll call him Eddie Intolerant) owed him $10,000,000!

Eddie admitted that his business had gone belly up and he couldn't pay the money back. The king, in a slight rage, ordered that the man and his family be put to work and all his possessions—his house, car, camper, jet skis, yes, everything he owned—be sold so the king could be repaid.

But Eddie fell down at the king's feet, begging His Majesty to be patient with him. He promised to pay it all back as soon as he could.

King Justly felt sorry for him, and compassion got the best of the king. He decided to forgive the man's debt and let him go.

But when Eddie left the palace, he pounced on his cousin Vinny, who owed him a few bucks. When his cousin couldn't pay, Eddie pressed charges and had him thrown into the clinker!

The news of Eddie Intolerant's harsh actions reached the palace, and the king was mighty mad! He sent for Eddie, gave him the once-over, took a deep breath, then let him have it!

"You evil-hearted wretch! Here I forgave you all that tremendous debt, just because you asked me to. Shouldn't you have mercy on others, just as I had mercy on you?"

The king was so peeved that he sent the man to solitary confinement until he paid back every single cent! Whoa!

In this parable that Jesus told in Matthew 18:23-35, patience and forgiveness are closely linked. We see the patience that the king had toward the man who owed him a ton of money. In his patience, he was filled with compassion and chose to forget about the debt—to wipe it away, to forgive the man! In turn, because he had been so merciful, he wanted the man to have patience toward others.

Same for us! Let's examine this connection.

God is patient with us. Because he is patient, he actually forgives our mess-ups, our mishaps, our major offenses. Look at this verse in the Old Testament:

> *"I am Jehovah, the merciful and gracious God," he said, "slow to anger and rich in steadfast love and truth. I, Jehovah, show this steadfast love to many thousands by forgiving their sins."*
>
> EXODUS 34:6, TLB

God is patient, therefore he forgives. Why is he patient? Because he loves us. It's that simple. And that simple truth has kept him from sending Jesus back to earth—he waits patiently, wanting everyone to wake up and come to their senses—to turn to Christ!

> *The Lord is not slow about His promise, as some count slowness, but is **patient** toward you, not wishing for any to perish but for all to come to repentance.*
>
> 2 PETER 3:9, NASB

God's patient forgiveness, flowing from a heart of love, is so incredible. Yet, it is not to be taken lightly. What if we don't take God seriously?

Paul had this discussion with the church at Rome. Let's eavesdrop!

Don't you realize how patient he is being with you? Or don't you care? Can't you see that he has been waiting all this time without punishing you, to give you time to turn from your sin? His kindness is meant to lead you to repentance.

ROMANS 2:4, TLB

Whoa! He goes on to say that those who patiently do what is pleasing to God will receive eternal life. But those who fight God's truth and do evil are going to get blasted!

Where are you? Are you following God's will? Is his patient love and kindness penetrating your heart and leading you to beg his forgiveness and repent of your sin? In turn, are you being patient with others? Don't risk being like Eddie Intolerant. Because the King of Kings himself has granted you patience, go ahead and grant it to others. Your patience will deem you a princess!

Beauty Builders

1. What did Eddie Intolerant ask of King Justly? Why do you think Eddie treated cousin Vinny the way he did? Is there someone you need to forgive? Who? Do it now!

2. Do problems and trials in life have a purpose? Read Romans 5:3-5 and James 1:2-4. How do you think patience helps to develop our character?

Day Four

Why Wait on God? Ask Sarah!

It was not a happy day in the life of Sarah. She just learned that her slave-girl, Hagar, had indeed become pregnant by *her* husband, Abraham. To make matters worse, Hagar was behaving pompously and rebelliously toward Sarah. Her in-your-face attitude only flamed Sarah's intolerant emotions. She fought back tears as she watched Hagar flaunting her swollen belly. It made the sting of her situation even worse. See, Sarah was barren. Childless.

Now God had promised Sarah and Abraham that he would grant them a child. But it had been so long. Years and years had passed. Sarah was exhausted from waiting! She reasoned that God had either forgotten her or that he must not have really meant that she would personally give birth. Perhaps God intended for Sarah's slave girl to have a child and give it to Sarah to raise as her own (that was a common practice back then).

Sarah's impatience caused her to take matters into her own hands. She devised her plan, presented it to Abraham and he consented. Sarah *gave* Hagar to Abraham for the purpose of conceiving a child!

But Hagar's son, Ishmael, was not God's chosen child for Abraham and Sarah. Sarah had given in to her own reasoning and jumped ahead of God's perfect timetable.

Did God finally make good on his promise to the childless couple? Yes! Isaac was born, a healthy little boy, but only after his mom and dad had waited nearly twenty-five years from the time of the promise!

We learn from Sarah that being impatient and trying to help

God along can really mess stuff up. You can read this story in Genesis 16 and 17.

Yes, waiting is hard! It requires restraint. It requires perseverance. It requires endurance.

We live in an impatient society. We have microwaves to quickly heat up our hot dogs and pop our popcorn. We have fast-food restaurants for quick meals and calculators to help us quickly add. We want *what* we want and we want it right now! We want something to happen, something to be over. We want out of our tight situations or to be set free from our discomforts. Waiting is inconvenient and uncomfortable!

That's what Sarah thought. That's what most people think. But what does God think? What's his take on waiting? Check out this verse:

> *Yet those who wait for the Lord/ Will gain new strength/ They will mount up with wings like eagles/ They will run and not get tired/ They will walk and not become weary.*
>
> ISAIAH 40:31, NASB

God's Word teaches us that waiting is definitely to our advantage! First, when we patiently wait, we gain new strength! God honors our patience by reaching down into our nearly empty energy supplies and filling us with new strength. He refreshes us. He gives us the "joy juice" that will keep us going. When we are weak, he can be strong through us.

Second, waiting helps us mount up with wings as eagles (see Isaiah 40:31). Eagles have the ability to spread their incredible wings, lock them into position, and soar for an incredible distance without having to flap themselves silly. When we wait on God and trust his timing in our tough situations, he will help us soar above the temptation to give up or to do it our own way.

Third, we will run and we will walk without slowing down to a crawl, then collapsing! Waiting strengthens our faith. See, when we are patient with our circumstances and with other people, we get to watch God work everything out. We experience him firsthand, which banishes doubt and boosts our faith. Now, that's worth waiting for!

Beauty Builders

1. Does something in your life seem to be *on hold* right now? Could it be that this is part of God's plan for you? Explain the situation and your feelings about waiting.

2. Have you ever done the Sarah thing, ever panicked and jumped ahead of God? What happened when you took matters into your own hands or what *could* happen if you choose to take matters into your own hands? Read Psalm 37:7-9.

Random Acts of Patience

Here are a couple cool clues to help you be perfectly patient:

✿ Surrender all your tough stuff to God.

✿ Trust God's timetable.

✿ Spend time with a younger sibling—you get to practice your patience.

✿ Look at others' lives through *their* eyes.

✿ Endure trials, don't hide from them.

✿ Minister to disabled children.

✿ Baby-sit.

✿ Listen to an elderly person tell you a story, again.

✿ Refuse to raise your voice.

"And patience develops strength of character in us and helps us trust God more each time we use it until finally our hope and faith are strong and steady."

ROMANS 5:4, TLB

Day Five

Getting Personal:
To Be or Not to Be ... Patient

If you were going to rate your level of patience where do you think you would be? Below average, average, or superior? Not sure? Use this quiz to find out!

Circle the answer that best describes the way you would react in the following situations:

1. You just found out that you were replaced as the yearbook editor because you missed the first deadline. Do you:
   a. Keep quiet, while secretly hoping the yearbook stinks.
   b. Accept responsibility for your actions and continue to work as an assistant.
   c. Have your parents call the principal and try to get the teacher to reinstate you, or else.

2. You're in the school cafeteria when you pop the tab on your soda and it sprays the front of your new shirt. Do you:
   a. Let a swear word slip out as you frantically dry yourself off.
   b. Take a deep breath, say, "I can't believe what just happened," and joke all day that you're wearing cola-scented cologne.
   c. Threaten to sue the careless soda delivery person who let the cans get shaken up.

3. Your elderly grandma moved in with your family two months ago. The family takes turns feeding and cleaning her up. You can't stand it one more minute. Do you:

    a. Get in and out as fast as you can, even if she has only eaten a little food.

    b. Ask the Lord to help you love her like he loves her and feel honored to care for her.

    c. Pay your brother to take your shift.

4. Your parents divorced two years ago. Your dad keeps breaking weekend plans with you to be with his girlfriend and her kids instead of you. Do you:

    a. Collapse on your bed, cry your eyes out, and refuse to leave your room the rest of the night.

    b. Tell him you'll just look forward to seeing him when he's available. Then pray and ask the Lord to show him how much you need him in your life.

    c. Tell him he needs to get his priorities straight and that you'll call him when you're good and ready to see him.

5. You have to be at band practice in exactly eight minutes and you're still in the orthodontist's chair across town! Do you:

    a. Hint to the dental hygienist that you're going to be in big trouble if you're not at band practice.

    b. Allow the dentist to finish adjusting your braces, thank him, go to band practice with a note from your mom, and endure your conductor's harsh remarks.

    c. Demand the dentist compensate you for the inconvenience.

6. *Someone has been stealing from the cash register at work. It always happens on your shift, but you've explained that it's not you. Your boss has just called you into his office for the third time.* Do you:
   a. Quit.
   b. Calmly explain once again that you would never steal and volunteer to take a lie detector test.
   c. Set a trap to find the real menace and get her fired.

7. *You've taken God's command very seriously to wait until marriage before having sex. But the guys at your school—even a few in your youth group—tease you about wearing a "true love waits" ring.* Do you:
   a. Remove the ring, but keep your commitment.
   b. Calmly smile and explain that living life God's way is worth it … and so is waiting.
   c. Verbally abuse them for being disrespectful pigs who only want girls for one thing—sex.

8. *Your mom is on a yelling rampage. She seems to be upset about something all the time.* Do you:
   a. Get in her face and ask her what her problem is.
   b. Politely do what she asks and then pray, asking God to help you understand what your mom is going through and why she's upset.
   c. Yell right back.

Scoring: If you answered mostly A's, you are being tolerant! As we discovered earlier this week, tolerance looks like patience, but it's not the real thing. You're teetering between pure patience and impatience. Let the Holy Spirit have full control in your life!

If you answered mostly B's, congrats! You are definitely traveling down the patience path. Keep it up!

If you answered mostly C's, uh-oh! Impatience has its claws deep in your flesh! Refuse to let the ugly flesh win! Turn from your testy tantrums and outrageous outbursts. Get into the Word—abide in the Vine, and allow the Lord's patience to flow through you.

Just don't grow impatient with your patience! Like the caterpillar that spins itself into a cocoon, then emerges as a breathtaking butterfly, all things take time. Keep growing into the gorgeous gal God wants you to become. Don't settle for being in the cocoon. Endure the process and emerge with elegance!

Beauty Builders

1. In what type of situations does it seem impossible for you to be patient?

2. Patience *is* possible! Put on your thinking cap and come up with four things that would help you become more patient.

3. Skim through everything you've learned this week about patience. Now, create a plan of action!

Heavenly Father,
I know firsthand that you are a patient God. I long to be like you! Fill me with your Spirit, that I might be elegantly even-tempered with the people and situations you have put in my life.

Teach me to wait on you and to resist the urge to take matters into my own hands. With your help, I, too, can mount up with wings as an eagle and soar.

Help me to understand and accept the fact that being patient helps to develop in me a godly strength of character. I want that, Lord! In Jesus' name, Amen.

Weekend Journal

Write a letter to God thanking him for his divine patience with you. Be specific. Follow this with a prayer inviting the Holy Spirit to do the work in your heart that will make you a more patient person.

Dear Heavenly Father,

With love,

_____

Chapter Six

Smashingly Sweet!

*The Beautiful Quality
of Kindness*

The Basic Ingredients of Kindness

"Kindnesses are Christlike acts that benefit others—even at your expense."
Carissa, 17

Mindy sat next to Allie every day in chemistry class. She never talked to her much, but lately she noticed Allie was cutting class a lot, and when she was there she was only *half* there. Her eyes stayed glued to the floor, her arms wrapped around her waist.

Feelings of compassion began to creep into Mindy's heart. What was wrong? Was there something she could do for Allie? She could at least offer to help her get caught up with chemistry! So she offered.

"Hi, Allie. Since you missed a few classes last week, would you like me to help you with the zillion assignments Mr. T. gave us?"

Allie stared at her. Then she shrugged.

Mindy took that as a yes and invited Allie to her house to study.

Mindy soon learned that Allie had a lot more than missed homework to handle. Allie's parents were fighting all the time and threatening to split up. The tension at home was tough on Allie and she couldn't concentrate on school or anything.

Mindy started inviting Allie to spend the night—a welcome reprieve from home. Mindy even changed her plans a few times just to be with Allie.

Mindy's other friends teased her, "Who are you trying to be, Mother Teresa?" But seeing Allie open up and actually laugh once in awhile made it worthwhile!

A kindhearted friend! That is who Mindy was trying to be. And she was quite good at it actually! Mindy's example shows us the BASIC INGREDIENTS of kindness. Check it out!

✿ *Mindy noticed!* True kindness pays attention to what's happening. Mindy was keen and sensitive to Allie's behavior and changing moods. Allie's class-cutting and body language clued Mindy in that something was up with Allie.

✿ *Mindy cared!* True kindness doesn't just notice; it cares! Mindy allowed her heart to be opened, and the Holy Spirit flooded it with compassionate care. Genuine care requires action!

✿ *Mindy stepped out!* True kindness gets out of its comfort zone and reaches out to those who are hurting. Mindy got involved … not just in Allie's homework, but in Allie's life! It wasn't always convenient, but Mindy chose to put Allie first.

✿ *Mindy risked rejection!* True kindness pushes past the fear of rejection or suspicion. Someone might wonder what you are doing or what you want from them! Continued, genuine kindness will prove you just want to help enhance another's life—even at your own expense!

✿ *Mindy felt fantastic!* True kindness in not a duty, it's a delight! If it's done out of obligation and your heart's not into it, it's not Spirit-filled kindness. Mindy didn't care what her friends said; she wanted to be kind to Allie. Her reward? A heartfelt blessing!

For we are to be kind to others, and God will bless us for it.
1 PETER 3:9, TLB

Beauty Builders

1. Which basic ingredient of kindness is hardest for you? Why? Which is easiest? Why?

2. Offer a kindness to someone who has hurt you. Responding in kindness is a truly gorgeous thing to do! So, who comes to mind? What did they do? What can you do for them?

Day Two

Sweet Sarcasm?

The headlines read, "Recovering the Lost Art of Kindness."

Today, in our society, it's almost expected that a person be impolite, disrespectful, foul-mouthed, mean, and just plain rude! (There's that ugly flesh again!)

That's the exact opposite of kindness!

But less than one hour of surfin' the channels on TV confirms that kindness is not cool in the eyes of an ungodly world. People are put down, picked on, verbally abused, and intentionally insulted. Unkind words are used to cut people to size.

How do audiences respond? With laughter! These unkindnesses are usually done so that they come off funny. I can't help but think that the Holy Spirit does not find them very humorous!

The number one way you can be kind to others is with your words. Guarding your words can bring real joy—maybe even a chuckle—to the Heavenly Trio.

God's Word gives us some guidelines as to what words not to let leak out of our mouths. Let these verses grab your attention (and your tongue)! Choose to use your ABC's to gravitate toward graciousness!

Snag a look at this line-up of Scriptures:

He who covers a transgression seeks love, but he who repeats a matter separates intimate friends.

PROVERBS 17:9, NASB

A lying tongue hates those it crushes, and a flattering mouth works ruin.

PROVERBS 26:28, NASB

Don't use bad language. Say only what is good and helpful to those you are talking to, and what will give them a blessing.

EPHESIANS 4:29, TLB

Stop being mean, bad-tempered and angry. Quarreling, harsh words, and dislike of others should have no place in your lives. Instead, be kind to each other.

EPHESIANS 4:31-32, TLB

Dirty stories, foul talk and coarse jokes—these are not for you. Instead, remind each other of God's goodness and be thankful.

EPHESIANS 5:4, TLB

Don't get involved in foolish arguments which only upset people and make them angry. God's people must not be quarrelsome.

2 TIMOTHY 2:23-24, TLB

But no human being can tame the tongue. It is always ready to pour out its deadly poison. Sometimes it praises our heavenly Father, and sometimes it breaks out into curses against men who are made like God. And so blessing and cursing come pouring out of the same mouth. Dear brothers, surely this is not right!

JAMES 3:8-10, TLB

The heart that is smashingly sweet will choose to stop speaking mean, evil, argumentative, harsh, gossipy, and lying words!

Someone who is smashingly sweet will use her words to build others up, not cut them down. Her tongue will speak blessing and not cursing. She will speak words of thankfulness as gratitude flows from her inner being.

So, swallow those juicy tidbits, quick comebacks, and sarcastic remarks! Let words of kindness come from your sweet heart, and help our world rediscover the lost art of kindness.

Beauty Builders

1. "Sticks and stones may break my bones, but words will never hurt me." Yeah, right! How have you been affected by someone's harsh words?

2. Reread the previous Scripture verses, then write a prayer asking the Lord to help you guard your tongue and to speak words of kindness and encouragement.

Day Three

Jesus: Never Too Busy to Care

Most of us jam-pack each twenty-four hour allotment with friends, classes, drivers' ed, babysitting, and shopping, not to mention the way we can burn up those phone lines!

Add it all up. What do you get?

A life that is too crowded for kindness.

Yep.

Our busy schedules pull the plug on our kindness potential!

Kindness takes time. It asks us to be available—not perfect, not know-it-alls—just available. Kindness asks us to stop long enough to care. It bids us to sit and listen.

Will we answer the call of kindness?

Jesus did.

Jesus was never too busy for anyone. He wasn't rushed, hurried, or late for an appointment. He made time to stop and talk.

Think of what it must have been like for the Samaritan woman. The local station, WSAM, was probably broadcasting the story! The lady was just there to draw water from the well. She had to do her work in the middle of the day when the sun was hot, since the other women who drew their water in the cool of the day despised her.

Enter Jesus. He spoke gently, asking for a drink.

Me? Are you talking to me? she thought. See, Jews didn't converse with Samaritans, especially female Samaritans! But Jesus reached out to her that warm summer day and changed her life forever (see John 4:1-39). Jesus was available. He stopped to care. He listened to her heart. He reached out in kindness.

Then there was the big fish fry with all those people. Thousands of them! They had been following Jesus for three days, feasting on his teachings, hanging on to every word. But it was time for them to return to their homes. The weekend super conference was over!

Just one little glitch. No food! How could Jesus send them home spiritually full, but physically empty? He couldn't! The disciples could have, however! "Where are we going to get enough food for all these folks? Think of the expense! It's just not doable." Blah, blah, blah. They were full of excuses.

Not Jesus.

He had compassion on the people. Out of the kindness of his heart, he took the seven loaves and three little fishes someone scrounged up and pulled off the biggest fish and chips feast ever! (See Mark 8:1-9.)

Yes, it was a miracle. Yes, it was a God-thing. Yet the lesson is for you and me. What was Jesus teaching? To be kind! To be moved to action! To let compassion compel you to stop and care, sit and listen!

One more example.

It's about feet. Dusty feet. Dirty toes. Smelly soles.

The lowest servant got this dirty deed: washing his master's feet! In this case, the Master is the one who got the towel, filled the basin with warm water, and began to cleanse the feet of his servants, his disciples (see John 13:1-17).

It was an act of kindness, of humility, of service. Jesus was leading by example, showing them that they, too, were to serve each other—to think no job too insignificant or beneath them. To be kind to one another.

Jesus was kind when he walked this earth two thousand years ago.

He's still kind today.

Will you follow his lead? Will you clear your schedule when kindness calls?

Beauty Builders

1. Jesus took time to be kind to everyone—regardless of age, stature, or social status! Read Mark 10:13-16. What insight does this give you about Jesus?

2. How do you feel when you know you have truly been heard? Do you struggle with really listening to others? Explain. Ask the Lord to help you learn to listen, and then express your gratitude that he always listens to you!

Learning to Listen

Listening is one of the greatest acts of kindness you can offer anyone these days. Listening causes us to open our hearts to those around us, to sense their pain, to step into their shoes.

It's a funny thing about listening. You don't have to have all the answers. Just your nod, your eye contact, your gentle touch is often all the response a person needs.

God gave you two ears and one mouth. Get the hint? We're to listen twice as much as we talk!

So take a deep breath, forget about yourself, and tune in to the other person. How very, very kind of you!

Day Four

The Servant-Hearted Shunamite

Mother Teresa once said that after years of working with the poor and sick people in India, she realized that being unwanted is the worst disease that any human being can ever experience.

Does that tug on your heartstrings? It does mine.

No one should feel unwanted. Yet, every day people exist without really living! They feel isolated, alone, and worthless. Many are homeless and hungry. That's a situation we can change!

We can be like the Shunammite woman! Her kindness to Elisha, this homeless, hungry prophet, was such a blessing.

Never heard of her?

Allow me to introduce you.

She lived in a village called Shunem and became known as the Shunammite.

She had heard of the wonders Elisha had performed. She was aware that he was the one responsible for the miracle oil in the widow's jars, making it possible for her to sell the oil and pay her debts (see 2 Kings 4:1-7). The Shunammite woman knew that Elisha was a holy man.

Pulling back the lace curtain from her window, she would see him pass by as he traveled through her region. She noted his weariness and was ready with food for him the next time he was within sight. How refreshing! How thoughtful!

After that, Elisha stopped at her home frequently. Her courage to reach out and be kind opened up a whole new friendship. Eventually, she spoke to her husband of a plan she had. He consented.

Excitement filled her as she awaited Elisha's next trip through town. She hoped her news would delight him. Indeed, it did! She had arranged to have a small chamber constructed for the prophet, a place where he could rest and be alone with God. A home away from home. Incredible! This woman was such a blessing to him!

The Shunammite woman was kind, thoughtful, polite, gracious, considerate, and charitable! All of these beautiful qualities caused her to be one more thing. A servant. Her story is in 2 Kings 4:8-37.

The Greek word for *kindness* can be translated as "useful." See, we are *kindness-in-action* when we help those in need. We are useful for the kingdom of God! You and I become God's hands and feet here on earth. He uses us to reach out to others. And when we do, it's like we're doing it *for him* and *to him*.

It's true!

But, hey, why take my word for it when you've got Jesus' word?

In another parable, Jesus shares with the boys about the King (that's him) separating the sheep (the righteous folks—that's the Christians) from the goats (yep, the ungodly).

He says to the righteous folks:

Come, you who are blessed by my Father; take your inheritance, the kingdom prepared for you since the creation of the world. For I was hungry and you gave me something to eat, I was thirsty and you gave me something to drink, I was a stranger and you invited me in, I needed clothes and you clothed me, I was sick and you looked after me, I was in prison and you came to visit me.

MATTHEW 25:34-36, NIV

The righteous scratched their heads and basically said, "Really? When did we do that?"

With gratitude in his eyes, the King replied, "Whatever you did for one of the least of these brothers of mine, you did it for me."

Cool, huh?

Donating your old clothes, serving at a soup kitchen, praying for your ill friends—these are more than just nice gestures. They are *you* being Jesus in the life of someone in need. It's *you* being just like the Shunammite woman. Kind to the core! There to care!

Beauty Builders

1. God always honors our kindness and rewards our obedience. Find out what he did for the Shunammite woman in 2 Kings 4:8-17. How do you think God's kindness to her affected her life, her faith? Now read verses 18-37 for the rest of the story!

2. Turn to Matthew 25:31-46 to get the full sheep and goat facts! What happened to the goats? What was the outcome of each? Who are you most like right now—the sheep or goats? Why?

Day Five

Getting Personal:
Checkin' Your Cool Acts of Kindness

You knew it was coming. And here it is! A humungo list of random acts of kindness! But wait. It's not just any old list. It's really a kindness quiz.

Here's the deal. Read through the list. If you committed any of these way-cool acts of kindness in the last twenty-four hours, you get a **WHOMPIN' 100 POINTS**! If you did them anytime in the last week, it's a **WONDERFUL 50 POINTS**! Sometime in the last six months, you get a **WIMPY 10 POINTS**. What? Some you've never done? Then there's not even one puny point for you, babe. **A FAT ZERO!** (Hey, at least this list will give you some great ideas.)

Just to show you how kind *I* am, fill in the last three slots with ideas of your own. (Hint: Make it something you've done so you rack up some extra points!)

Now grab your pen and get going!

____ Let family members know you're praying for them— only if you really are, of course!

____ Help a friend do a chore—clean out the garage or rake the leaves together!

____ Say hi to a lonely-looking girl at school.

____ Volunteer to make dinner—even if it's just macaroni and cheese or frozen pizza.

____ Bake your favorite cookies and take them to one of your classes at school.

____ Let someone else be first in line at the video store or grocery store or fast-food restaurant.

_____ Ask a new person or one who's shy to sit with you at youth group.

_____ Skip your workout to help a friend with homework.

_____ Wash the family car.

_____ Invite a brother or sister to shoot hoops with you or play some sport or game.

_____ Give up the last 15 minutes of your favorite show to take a call from your grandma.

_____ Shock your mom by dusting, vacuuming, or picking up around the house.

_____ Give someone special something that means a lot to you.

_____ Make someone a friendship bracelet.

_____ Say something encouraging to someone.

_____ Hug your dad.

_____ Donate clothes you don't need to a local homeless shelter.

_____ Serve at a soup kitchen.

_____ Be a hero and do one of your sibling's chores.

_____ Treat someone the way you would want to be treated.

_____ Visit a shut-in or someone in a nursing home.

_____ Be a children's Sunday school assistant.

_____ Give your mom a big kiss on the cheek.

_____ Write a note of encouragement to someone—a teacher, youth pastor, pastor, a friend's mom who always gives you a ride!

_____ Tell someone about Jesus.

_____ Spend time with a kid from a single-parent home.

_____ Clean up your room and make your bed.

_____ Baby-sit for free.

_____ Let a family member have the TV remote for a night.

____ Sit and listen to someone.

____ Celebrate a birthday—send a card, a small gift.

____ Buy someone a soft drink.

____ Shine your dad's shoes.

____ Hug a sibling.

____ Compliment your mom or dad on dinner.

____ Write a note of appreciation or admiration to someone.

____ Help raise money for a charity.

____ Your own: _____

____ Your own: _____

____ Your own: _____

OK, get out your calculator and start adding! How did you do? Out of a possible four thousand points, where are you on the kindness scale?

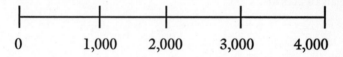

How does your score make you feel?

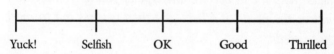

If you're like me, you have some definite room for improvement. Isn't it great to have the Holy Spirit in us to nudge us when we hesitate to be smashingly sweet to others?

He wants us to remember that we are reaching out in Jesus' name. And, people are not interruptions in our busy schedules, they are opportunities to minister kindness.

Beauty Builders

1. In what type of situation is it most challenging for you to be kind?

2. Think of three things you could do to become a kinder kind of gal.

3. Based on all you've learned this week about kindness, create a plan of action.

Heavenly Father,
Even though I live in a world that is impolite and unkind,
please help me to become the type of young woman who
notices the needs of others and then reaches out to meet
those needs.

In your name, I offer you my words to encourage, my
hands to help, my arms to hug, my ears to listen, and my
heart to be moved to action by your compassion. And
remind me, Lord, that when I'm kind to someone, it's the
same as being kind to you. In Jesus' name, Amen.

Weekend Journal

Because thy lovingkindness is better than life
    my lips will praise Thee.
So I will bless thee as long as I live
    I will lift up my hands in thy name.

PSALM 63:3-4, NASB

As a letter to God, rewrite this psalm in your own words, expressing your thoughts about the Lord's kindness and your reaction to it. Then ask him to help you extend the same kindness to others that he has shown to you.

Dear Heavenly Father,

With love,

Chapter Seven

Passionately Pure!

*The Beautiful Quality
of Goodness*

It's Totally a God-Thing

*"Goodness is knowing the pure and
right response, then doing it."*
Annie, 14

Ah, goodness. The beautiful quality of the Holy Spirit that shows up in us and shines out onto others.

It's a funny thing about this quality. Goodness can bring joy to some and judgment to others. When we shine with goodness, our presence can make some people uncomfortable. The presence of God in us exposes their bad attitudes, their selfish desires, and their hidden sin. It's called conviction. It's on the top of the Holy Spirit's to-do list.

To others, like those who are hurting, hopeless, and helpless, our presence is comforting. They know we will lend a hand, act justly, offer support, help them stand strong. They know we will do the right thing, because we want to do good and be good just like the God we serve.

Goodness is totally a God-thing.

Yep. The Greek word for goodness that is used in the Bible is not found in secular writings. It is a word reserved for God. It is a word reserved for those who let God's nature live through them.

Hopefully, that includes you!

Like an ice-cream sundae dripping with chocolate sauce, the Bible is overflowing with sweet Scriptures on goodness—referring to a good nature (godlike character) and good deeds (godlike actions)!

Let's narrow the focus. Let's talk moral goodness. Purity. Righteous living. We live in a backward society that says bad is good and good is bad. And that disgusts God (see Proverbs 17:15).

One message today that screams at us is that sex before marriage is a good thing. Wrong. It's definitely not a good thing. The Bible tells us that God's will is for us to abstain from sexual immorality (see 1 Thessalonians 4:3). Our Father (who invented sex, by the way) knows what is best! Wholesomeness. Purity. Virginity!

Lots of girls today are wearing purity rings or necklaces to remind themselves of their pledge to sexual purity. Girlfriend, *you* are worth the wait! And God is worth obeying!

Another aspect of moral goodness is honesty. Ever see peers cheat on tests? Lie to their parents? Swipe something? Society sees those as little offenses, if offenses at all! But to God, sin is sin. All of it rots, in his opinion!

God desires truth clear down to the center of our being! (See Psalm 51:6.) Total honesty. God despises lying. He wants us to be truthful. To know the truth and to speak the truth (see Proverbs 6:16-17).

That can be pretty tough in a world that teaches that truth is relative. Ever heard someone say, "Well, if it works for you, then it's OK." Huh? "Whatever it is, if it makes you happy, it must be alright." Huh?

The world teaches there are no moral absolutes. No rights or wrongs. No sins. FALSE! We serve a good God who has set forth moral absolutes. Where do we find these absolutes? In the book. The Bible. The ultimate truth. The absolute truth. Guidelines for moral goodness to govern our lives.

With the goodness of God residing in us through the Holy Spirit, we have the privilege and the responsibility to take a stand for what is morally good and right. To stand on the truth of God's Word.

So, what happens when *you* walk into a class or a party? Do you make some people uncomfortable because of your moral choices?

If so, that's a *good* thing!

Beauty Builders

1. Why does God not want you to pollute yourself with immoral things like sex, drunkenness, bad language, crass jokes, and lies? Find out in Romans 6:13. Then read 1 Corinthians 6:19-20. What do these verses mean to you?

2. Some people will want you to feel bad for being good. Read 1 Peter 3:13-17. Have you ever suffered for standing up for what was right? What is the value of a good conscience?

Day Two

A Goody-Goody Girl
in a Bad-Girl World

Sometimes she hated it. The sneers. The jokes. The name-calling. But, honestly, she wouldn't have it any other way.

Tess was a goody-goody. She knew it, and so did everyone else. She was known for being polite, for refusing to be bribed into sharing her test answers, for never drinking at parties, for heading up the Adopt-a-Grandparent project at the nursing home, and for starting the on-campus Bible club. She even prayed at the school flagpole!

Can you identify with Tess? I can. In high school and in college, I was known for being a goody-two-shoes. Yes, some made fun of me, but others respected me for my beliefs.

That's OK. We're supposed to be goody-goodies! Want proof?

Christian women should be noticed for being kind and good, not for the way they fix their hair or because of their jewels or fancy clothes.

1 TIMOTHY 2:9, TLB

We're to be noticed for being what? Kind and good! God has called us to goodness.

Get comfy, snuggle down, and go back with me to the very beginning.

Scene One: In the beginning God created, well, everything! And after he created it, what did he say? "It is GOOD!" God gave himself an atta boy! Then he created mankind, to which he spouted, "Oh, VERY good!" (I'm not kidding! Read Genesis 1:31.)

Scene Two: God was about to leave Adam and Eve alone in Eden, but first, he warned them not to—nada, no way—eat of the tree in the middle of the garden, the tree of the knowledge of good and evil. Why? Because God never wanted his beloved creations to experience evil! (See Genesis 2:16-17.)

Scene Three: Slithering Satan, disguised as a snake, convinces Eve to do a little taste testing. With that first bite, an act of disobedience to God (yep, sin!), evil entered the world of Adam and Eve. They got booted out of the garden and separated from their holy God! (Check out Genesis, chapter 3.)

Scene Four: God sends Jesus into the world to pay the sin debt of man and bring goodness back into the world!

The End
(OK, it was the short version!)

In and of ourselves, we are not good. But with the Holy Spirit living in us, goodness is camped out in our hearts!

Therefore, it's our job to be kind and good! Yep, we've been given the assignment of overcoming evil with good (see Romans 12:21). Evil is the opposite of goodness.

God says:

- Hate what is evil; cling to what is good (see Romans 12:9, NIV).
- Turn your back on evil (see Proverbs 3:7, TLB).
- Seek goodness (see Proverbs 11:27).

How do we overcome evil? By understanding two things.

First, the Holy Spirit living *in* you is greater than the force of evil in this world (see 1 John 4:4).

Second, you were designed to do good deeds. As proof, read:

For we are God's workmanship, created in Christ Jesus to do good works, which God prepared in advance for us to do.
EPHESIANS 2:10, NIV

Our purpose in life is to do good deeds. The goody-two-shoes title fits, so wear it!

When you're abiding in the Vine, goodness will fill your soul and shine out through your actions. So, when it comes to goodness, just do it!

Beauty Builders

1. Light (or goodness) exposes the evil deeds of darkness. Read Philippians 2:15. In the midst of a _____ and _____ generation you can shine like a _____. Think of three ways you can shine at school this week.

2. You can impact your world for Christ! What will happen when others see your good deeds? Find the answer in Matthew 5:14-16. What do you think will happen if you choose not to light your corner of the world?

Random Acts of Goodness

Hide it under a bushel? No way! Let your light shine!

✿ Gather up all your friends to pray at See You at the Pole.

✿ Start a True Love Waits campaign on your campus.

✿ Study the gospels—find out WWJD and do it!

✿ Do whatever the Holy Spirit whispers in your ear.

✿ Memorize Bible verses.

✿ Become a candy striper and help out at your local hospital.

✿ Stop a vicious rumor!

✿ Don't lie.

✿ Volunteer at a children's shelter—reading to kids, playing games, rocking babies.

✿ Don't laugh at dirty jokes.

✿ Distribute pamphlets against abortion.

✿ Choose purity over popularity.

✿ Do to others what you would want them to do to you!

Let us not become weary in doing good, for at the proper time we will reap a harvest if we do not give up.

GALATIANS 6:9, NIV

Day Three

Jesus: Not Your Average Shepherd

Baa. Baa. The sound of bleating sheep. Music to the shepherd's ears. Proof he is doing his job well.

The sheep are grazing in green pastures, eating their little hearts out. They are happy little guys as they sip from the still water where the shepherd has led them (sheep can't drink from a rushing stream).

Those woolly creatures are confident and comfortable in the shepherd's care. They trust him to protect them from robbers and wolves, lightening and hail, flies and snakes.

They have come to realize that if they wander off, the shepherd will come to find them. And with the crook of his staff, he will lead them back to the flock.

The sheep are continually within the shepherd's reach, and within the sound of his voice. Yep. The sheep know the voice of their shepherd. When they hear the call of a neighboring shepherd, they do not respond. It is only the voice of their herdsman that catches their attention. They know their shepherd and he knows them. In fact, he knows them by name!

Gee, what a GOOD shepherd!

This relationship between a shepherd and his sheep is the same one that Jesus uses to describe his relationship with his followers!

In fact, he calls himself the Good Shepherd in John 10:1-18, 25-30. This entire passage gives us a glorious glimpse into the goodness of our Savior. The exciting thing is that *we* get to be the recipients of his goodness!

Let's take a closer look.

Our Good Shepherd ...

Provides for us! Jesus provides everything we need! Air, water, rain, sunshine, shelter, food (OK, maybe you didn't like your mom's meatloaf last night, but you didn't go hungry, did you?)!

Protects us! Jesus sends his angels to watch over us, and the power of his name keeps us from the harmful hand of Satan. We can be free from fear! And even if, like the sheep, we go wandering off, he brings us back, for we are always within his reach. We are loved!

Possesses us! That's right. We are his prize possessions and he is intimately acquainted with us. With daily interaction, we develop a very personal relationship with our Shepherd; so close that he calls us by name. And we recognize his voice and follow him. Where does he lead us? Always along the best paths, full of goodness. He's a Shepherd we can trust!

Paid for us! Jesus said the Good Shepherd lays down his life for his sheep! That's what he did for us! We are so precious to him that he died so we could live with him forever in eternity!

Pampers us! The goodness of our Shepherd just doesn't stop! He has come to give his sheep—not just life—but ABUNDANT life (see verse 10). Does that mean a big house, fancy car, cool clothes, and all that? Not even close! The abundant life Jesus offers is far more satisfying than material objects. He knows our true needs! He offers us good gifts that satisfy our inner desires. Love. Joy. Peace. Patience. Kindness. Goodness. Faithfulness. Gentleness. Self-Control. Our Shepherd fills us with the beautiful qualities of himself. *That's* abundant living!

Beauty Builders

1. Take a second to reflect on each of the ways Jesus is the Good Shepherd in your life. Which one is most important to you? Why?

2. It's great to be a sheep! That's because the Spirit of the Good Shepherd lives in his sheep. Therefore, we, too, possess goodness. Just like Jesus, you can share your goodness with others. Think of five ways to do just that!

Gorgeous Girl Profile
Miss Karen McGregor

To nineteen-year-old Karen McGregor, a horse is a girl's best friend! Especially when that horse is a gift from God! Who would have guessed that God would lavish his goodness on a teenage girl in this fashion?

Not Karen!

But it really happened! Karen had been saving money for years to buy the one thing she wanted more than anything else, a horse. She worked with her dad as a carpenter's assistant, baby-sat, and did odd jobs—just to raise the cash. She had finally raised $1,500 and was on the lookout for a horse to call her own!

But then it happened. She received her *Brio* magazine in the mail and learned of an all-girl mission trip to Bolivia. Karen clearly sensed that God wanted her to go—but it would cost her not only ALL the money she had saved, but also her dream of owning a horse.

Karen had a strong, trusting relationship with God, and she answered his call. She was Bolivia-bound!

The trip was an unforgettable experience for Karen. She came face to face with poverty, played with children in orphanages, and told others about God's love. Yet what happened next *really* blew her away!

The mom of another *Brio* reader read about Karen's decision to obey God—even if it meant no horse! This mom, Rebecca Nielsen, was overwhelmed! She, at age fifteen, had worked hard to buy her first horse, and now owns a beautiful horse ranch. She, too, felt God speaking to her!

Rebecca flew Karen to her horse ranch and gave her the horse of her choice!

Incredible! Unbelievable! But soooo is God!

Karen—and you and I—serve a God who is good! He loves to give good gifts to his children—not because they deserve them or earned them, but because he loves them!

Karen obeyed the nudging of God to go and serve him in Bolivia. And God sent a thank-you gift—a really good one!

Every good thing bestowed and every perfect gift is from above, coming down from the Father of lights.

JAMES 1:17, NASB

Day Four

Behind the Scenes With Dorcas, Abbie, and da Queen

People who are filled with the goodness of God can't keep from doing good things.

Case in point, Miss Dorcas! Dorcas was from the seaport city of Joppa. Many poor families and women who lost their husbands at sea lived there. Dorcas "was always doing good and helping the poor" (Acts 9:36, NIV).

She was known for her seamstress abilities! No doubt she stitched dresses and tunics for those of little means. She made robes, coats, and perhaps even blankets for babies and quilts to warm the elderly. The goodness in her heart motivated her to reach out and bless others with her good deeds.

Another grand example of goodness is Abigail. She knew that her husband, Nabal, had greatly offended David and his men who had voluntarily protected her husband's sheep. But when they asked for food to satisfy their growing hunger, Nabal said no.

David was angry and Abigail knew it. She quickly prepared a feast for David and his men and personally delivered it to them. Her good deed was taken as an offering of peace. Her noble and charitable spirit won her David's respect. But that's not all. Later, when Abigail's husband died, David took her to be his wife! Huh! Her goodness won David's heart, too (see 1 Samuel 25).

Another noble woman of goodness was Queen Vashti. At least in *my* opinion! Following a seven-day feast, her tipsy husband ordered her to put on her crown and come to parade her beauty before his drunken guests. She refused. I respect that. She did not want to be the object of man's lust. Now, I realize she disobeyed her husband, and he stripped her of her title, but she stood up for purity and refused to be abused.

Besides, Queen Vashti's refusal to play along with her hubby opened the door for Esther to become queen! Esther was God's chosen woman to save the Jewish people from being destroyed (see Esther 1). Dorcas, Abigail, and Queen Vashti were each examples of goodness.

Jesus, knowing that people learn by example, shared a story with his disciples that focused on a person's goodness. It is a wonderful example for us to follow. It's the parable of the Good Samaritan. Flip open and read the story in Luke 10:30-37.

Two men who walked along the road ignored the man who was attacked, beaten, and robbed. But the third man, the Samaritan, stopped to help. He probably used the hem of his own garment to bandage the man's wounds! He laid the man on his own donkey while he unselfishly walked to the nearest inn. Then he paid the innkeeper to care for the man until he came back from his journey.

Here was a man full of goodness. It cost him his time, his personal belongings, and his money! The mercy he showed is an example for all of us to follow.

Doing good for others can be inconvenient and costly. Yet, when you love the Lord your God with all your heart, soul, and mind, you will be motivated to act on your feelings of compassion and do good unto others.

Need some help with that motivation factor?

First, whatever situation presents itself, ask yourself, "What would Jesus do?" The Bible tells us specifically that Jesus went around "doing good" (see Acts 10:38). Therefore, you can bet he'd do something good.

Second, let good thoughts get a grip on your attitudes, and your attitudes will lead you to good actions! Grab a glance at this:

Fix your thoughts on what is true and good and right. Think about things that are pure and lovely, and dwell on the fine, good things in others. Think about all you can praise God for and be glad about.

PHILIPPIANS 4:8, TLB

It's true that thoughts lead to attitudes and attitudes influence actions! When you fill yourself with thoughts that are passionately pure, your actions will be gloriously good!

Beauty Builders

1. Like Dorcas, Abigail, and Queen Vashti, are you known for your goodness? Does your family appreciate your good deeds? They will after you come up with five good deeds to do for them!

2. How can asking the WWJD question help you to grow in goodness?

Day Five

Getting Personal:
Pass the Salt, Please!

Are you salty or unsalty? No, I'm not talking about your popcorn, I'm talking about you!

Not sure?

Let's start by finding out exactly what salt does! Test your knowledge with this mini-quiz!

True False

☐   ☐   1. Salt causes foods to spoil.

☐   ☐   2. Salt has no effect on ice.

☐   ☐   3. Salt, like a spice, adds flavor.

☐   ☐   4. Gargling with salt water helps heal a sore throat.

☐   ☐   5. Salt makes a person thirsty.

(Answers: 1-F, 2-F, 3-T, 4-T, 5-T)

Did that help? Now do you know if you're salty? Does your life fit the description of this flavorful substance?

"So what if it does or doesn't?" you may be asking!

Jesus said you are the salt of the earth! Salt is good! When salt has lost its flavor and its effectiveness, it loses its goodness.

Catchin' on?

If you're salty, your goodness is showing. It's adding flavor. It's preserving! It's healing! It's even melting! And most important, your actions and reactions of goodness are making people thirst for God! Cool, huh?

Take this salty survey to see if your goodness is growin' and showin'.

Salt adds flavor. Does your presence add a sense of warmth and acceptance, or coolness and bitterness? Do you liven up the place, bringing zest, zip, and extra spice to others' lives? Do you dress and behave in good taste?

Salt preserves. Do you keep others' attitudes from spoiling something for everyone else? Do your well-seasoned words help get your peers' thoughts out of the gutter and onto good things?

Salt brings healing. Do you step in and help patch up broken friendships or mend misunderstandings in your home? Do you help those who have sinned to restore their relationship with God and get back on track?

Salt melts ice. Do your gentle responses dissolve the anger in others? Does the godly love you give to others melt their cold hearts?

Salt causes thirst. Does the way you handle situations cause others to notice you are a Christian? When you restrict your movies, magazines, language, and partying to levels that honor God, do others want to know why? When your WWJD bracelet or true-love-waits ring becomes an opportunity to stand up for what's right, do you speak the truth in love? Does your dedication to church and your youth group make your classmates ask about your beliefs?

The survey is now completed. Circle the results! You are:

Salty   Unsalty

The cool thing about being a Christian is that even if you're a little light on the salt, you *can* increase your flavor!

When real salt loses its flavor, when its taste goes flat, it's useless. It's not good for anything!

You don't have to be tasteless. You can grow to be intensely salty and full of goodness! It's simple to be salty (not always easy, but the steps are simple).

1. Stay clean. Yep, shake all the dirt out of your life using 1 John 1:9, and be pure.
2. Be serious. Well, about God, that is! Have a daily devotional time, pray, and read the Word.
3. Say yes! When the Holy Spirit prompts you to do or say something good, do it!

Follow these three steps and you'll be good and salty!

Beauty Builders

1. In what type of situations does it seem the hardest for you to display pure goodness?

2. What do you think would help you win in the goodness game? What changes do you need to make in your life?

3. Skim through this chapter. Seeing everything you've learned about goodness, create a plan of action!

Heavenly Father,

So often I feel so far from good. In fact, I question if there is any goodness in me at all! Then I remember you. You have sent your Holy Spirit in me to supply me with all of your goodness. It's in me! Help it to grow and take over and spread everywhere—like a really wild weed.

Father, don't let a day go by that I don't show goodness to someone in some way. I want to be a goody-goody, because it glorifies you! And may that goodness make others want to know why I do what I do. Then I can tell them about you! You are so good to me. In Jesus' name, Amen.

Weekend Journal

If you were going to e-mail God and thank him for his goodness in your life, what would you say? In what ways has he been good to you? Write it here:

Dear Heavenly Father,

With love,

_____

Chapter Eight

Lusciously Loyal!

*The Beautiful Quality
of Faithfulness*

Through Thick and Thin

"Being faithful is being like Christ—
constant and unchanging."
Hillary, 15

Let me ask you a question. What is one of the most valuable characteristics of friendship? OK, you're right! The chapter title gave it away! It's faithfulness. Loyalty!

Let's see if I can stump you on this one. What is the color of faithfulness? Ha! True-blue! Gotcha on that one!

Faithfulness is a rare and precious gem in our fickle and fancy-free world. Exactly what is faithfulness? It's standing strong in the middle of crummy circumstances! It's having integrity and sticking with things you start! It's keeping your promises!

The beautiful quality of faithfulness is one of the Holy Spirit's main attractions. That's 'cause being faithful affects nearly every area of our lives—our homework, grades, jobs, sports, and friendships! Being a faithful friend goes much further than a bunch of good intentions. It's about sticking it out through thick and thin!

Just ask Nann Chafin.

Nann is not an ordinary teen girl. She is an eighteen-year-old Southern belle with a gorgeous smile, warm and outgoing personality, and no hair! It's true. She has an autoimmune deficiency that makes her body think it is allergic to her hair. It's called alopecia areata.

As Nann's hair thinned and bald spots appeared, she started wearing hats to school. But cruel kids would pull them off. Others would laugh. Some just stared.

As if living without her hair wasn't enough of a crisis for a teen girl, Nann started noticing she was living without real friends, too. No one saved a seat for her at lunch anymore. They'd make plans, leaving her out. Eventually, the phone stopped ringing. In a recent interview with *Brio* magazine, Nann shared that at times like this you really find out who your true friends are!

"Some people let go of their friendship with me. I think they finally got too frustrated trying to understand what was going on in my life. They just didn't accept it."

Faithfulness was a quality that Nann's former friends lacked. (You'll be happy to know that God has given Nann lots of new friends over the past few years!)

It hurts to constantly be let down, lied to, and left out!

To be faithful friends we need to hang in there with others. We prove our friendship with our consistency and devotion.

Sometimes being faithful and true is inconvenient and totally uncomfortable.

Like when you've promised to keep a secret, but you realize your friend is in trouble. Maybe she's super-depressed. Maybe she's too hot with her boyfriend. Maybe she's taking laxatives or refusing to eat. Maybe she's being abused.

There *are* times when being a loyal friend means getting help. True friends stick by you through whatever happens.

Faithfulness in friendships is more than a nice thing, it's a necessity!

Beauty Builders

1. How have your friends and family been faithful to you? Unfaithful? How did each make you feel?

2. Why do you think faithfulness is important in the beauty quality line-up?

The Bible's Top Ten Tips for Building Better Friendships

1. *Be an encourager!* . . . . Ecclesiastes 4:9-10
2. *Be loyal!* . . . . Proverbs 16:28
3. *Be willing to lay down your life!* . . . . John 15:13
4. *Be available for counsel!* . . . . Proverbs 27:9
5. *Be loving!* . . . . 1 Corinthians 13:4-7
6. *Be a gossip stopper!* . . . . Proverbs 17:9
7. *Be there at all times!* . . . . Proverbs 17:17
8. *Be truthful!* . . . . Proverbs 27:5-6
9. *Be willing to confront (in love)!* . . . . Proverbs 27:17
10. *Be forgiving!* . . . . Matthew 18:21-22

Day Two

Fickle and Fancy-free

Teri put down the phone and just stood there for a minute. This had to be the fourth, no, fifth time in the last few months that Jodee had canceled their plans. She was so impulsive! Jodee just did whatever she wanted to, whenever she wanted.

Lindsey was wearing a promise ring from Rob. She usually rubbed their romance in everyone's faces. Then came camp. Lindsey met Josh. Off came the ring, until camp was over. Then she was all Rob's again. Lindsey was untrue.

Kim told her mom she would fold the clean laundry. It awaited her there in the basket, but she wasn't in the mood. She was tired. She'd do it ... sometime. Or else, maybe, just maybe, she could talk her younger brother Shawn into doing it. Laziness was getting the best of Kim.

There are many rivals to the beautiful quality of faithfulness. While you are working on becoming lusciously loyal, better be on guard!

Yep! Beware of fickle impulses! Dodge the temptation to be untrue. Don't let laziness creep in. Attack apathy face-to-face. Drop disloyalty on its head.

Sure, it's easier to be unfaithful. Yet God (who is 100 percent faithful and wants us to be like him) has planted faithfulness in our spirit. He has called us to be true. He invites us to be faithful and to join him at his Faithful Gala! It's a special luncheon where we can learn how to be loyal. As with any invitation, the specifics are spelled out for you.

You Are Invited

What: God's Faithful Gala!

Where: In the private chambers of your heart!

When: Now and forever!

Why: To learn the value of living a faithful life.
To become more like the Father.
To build relationships based on trust.
To reap the benefits of being faithful.

How: By loving the Lord with all your heart, soul, and mind, and by putting him first in everything you do!

RSVP
The GOD hotline (tell him all about it!)

What will your RSVP be? God rewards those who live a life of faithfulness. Let your eyes linger on this list!

- Be faithful and you'll be bowled over with blessings! (see Proverbs 28:20).
- When you're faithful in small ways, God will trust you with greater things! (see Matthew 25:21).
- When you are faithful, you are useful in the ministry! (see 2 Timothy 2:2).
- God personally protects us when we are faithful and true! (see Psalm 31:23).

Listen to the ways God has rewarded the faithfulness of two teen girls.

Patti says: "I've made it a priority to meet with God on a regular basis. It's not the same time everyday, in fact, it's four times a week! It's a commitment that has really blessed me. I've seen God strengthen me, teach me, and draw me closer to him. There's no better place to be."

Tyler says: "My friend has been very closed to church and hearing about Christ. Yet, I have continued to eat with her at lunch, meet her at the basketball games, and invite her to spend the night. My faithfulness paid off! She actually asked if she could come to youth group with me, and she finally opened her heart to God!"

Being faithful has its blessings and its rewards. But the best news of all is that you don't have to force yourself to do it! The Spirit of God within you gives you the desire and the ability to follow faithful's lead.

Beauty Builders

1. Which rival of faithfulness is threatening to move in and cause a meltdown: laziness, apathy, impulsiveness, or disloyalty? What can you to do to fight back?

2. What is your personal response to God's invitation to faithfulness? Why do you think God rewards our faithfulness?

Gorgeous Girl Profile
Miss Kersta Johnson

A couple of weeks ago, a lady named Judy Howard stayed with my family as she was walking across America for Jesus Christ. She was talking to me one night about how often she gives money to people she meets along the road, if they need it more than she does.

She also said that when she left on her trip, she had four hundred dollars, and she still had around four hundred dollars, because God always finds ways to provide for her.

One night, I thought I heard God telling me to give some money to Judy. I wasn't sure I wanted to do this, because I really wanted to buy new clothes or something with the twenty dollars that I had. But God kept telling me to give the money to Judy.

One morning I had left for school and also said good-bye to Judy, because she was moving on. I was bummed that she had to leave and even more disappointed when I got to school and realized that I had kept the twenty dollars.

I said a quick prayer telling God that if he really wanted me to give Judy this money, then he would need to provide me with another opportunity.

When I got home from school, Judy was still there! Because the weather was bad, she stayed an extra day.

Even though it was hard for me to keep my promise, I remained faithful to God and gave Judy the money. I felt great about what I did, and I'm sure it was the right thing. The whole situation reminded me of one of my favorite verses. It says, "For I can do everything God asks me to with the help of Christ who gives me the strength and power" (Philippians 4:13, TLB). It's so true!

Random Acts of Faithfulness

The facts are in! Faithfulness rocks! Check these out:

❀ Don't make commitments you can't keep.

❀ Get an accountability partner to help you.

❀ Do your chores and keep curfew!

❀ Whether others are watching or not, do your assignments as unto the Lord.

❀ Don't quit.

❀ Stop thinking someone else will pick up the slack or do your job for you!

❀ Understand that others are counting on you. Be there for them, just like God is there for you.

❀ Forget your feelings, just follow through.

❀ Place yourself in positions that require dedication, which will help develop your faithfulness.

❀ Go the extra mile.

Be faithful, even to the point of death, and I will give you the crown of life.

REVELATION 2:10, NIV

Day Three

God's Photo Album

Throughout the Bible we see pictures of God's faithfulness in the lives of his children.

Come closer.

Let's open his photo album of faith and take a peek at some of those snapshots.

Oh, look, it's Joseph! When he was a young man, God gave Joseph a dream. Joe was so excited, he went and shared it with his brothers. In the dream Joseph was a great ruler and his brothers were bowing down to him.

A dream? His brothers thought it was a nightmare! They captured little Joe and sold him into slavery. He served in the house of the Egyptian Pharaoh, where he did well and got promoted. Then Potiphar's (an Egyptian officer) wife took notice of him (Joe was a handsome dude), but when he refused her advances she was offended and accused him of rape. He was thrown into prison!

This picture is not looking so pretty! But hang on, God is faithful! God used Joseph to interpret the Pharaoh's dream, and Pharaoh yanked him out of that cell and crowned him ruler of Egypt. God never left Joseph.

Oh, yeah, about his brothers. They were hungry (there was a famine in the land) and came to Egypt to beg food, and who did they discover was in charge? Joseph! God was faithful to fulfill Joe's dream and he was faithful to provide food to his brothers, God's chosen people! (See Genesis 37–50.)

Whew!

Hey, there's a picture of Daniel. Yep, he's the one thrown into the lions' den because he refused to worship anyone or anything other than God! He was faithful to God. God was faithful to him. What happened in the lions' hangout? Nothing. God sent an angel to shut the lions' mouths. (See Daniel 6.)

Hey, that's a fine-looking couple—oh, it's Abraham and Sarah! God had promised to make Abraham the father of many nations. And he was faithful to keep his word. It took a little longer than the couple expected, that's all, but their faith in their faithful God remained strong.

Great pictures!

God's nature is to be faithful. He *can't* be unfaithful—it's not in him! But, let's let his Word speak for him:

> *Know therefore that the Lord your God is God; he is the faithful God, keeping his covenant of love to a thousand generations of those who love him and keep his commands.*
>
> DEUTERONOMY 7:9, NIV

> *But the Lord is faithful, and he will strengthen and protect you from the evil one.*
>
> 2 THESSALONIANS 3:3, NIV

> *Let us hold unswervingly to the hope we profess, for he who promised is faithful.*
>
> HEBREWS 10:23, NIV

That's three verses out of about three trillion! Is there any doubt left in your mind? God is faithful!

But, is he still faithful to us when we have been unfaithful to him? Yep. Incredible, huh?

Even when our faith fails, God stays faithful. Why? Because that's the way he is, and he can't be anything less than himself (see 2 Timothy 2:13). He is unchanging! *That* is a solid foundation for us to build our faith and our lives upon.

Beauty Builders

1. How can we know for sure that the Lord will remain faithful to us? Read Hebrews 13:8. Have you been unfaithful? Search your heart and confess your unfaithfulness. Then read 1 John 1:9.

2. Because God is faithful to his word, you can confidently build your life on him! Read Matthew 7:24-27. What is the benefit of building on the rock?

Chick Chat

Tell us about God's faithfulness to you!

When I was five years old, my dad developed cancer. It was treated and cured, but four years later, it reappeared, even worse than the first time. For several months, I lived with my aunt and uncle six hundred miles away from my home in St. Louis, while my dad lay dying in a hospital bed. The doctors gave my dad very little chance to live. But our church family prayed fervently for my dad. You can imagine the doctors' amazement when my dad began making significant progress, which eventually led to complete healing. I often think about how the doctors told my dad that he'd never walk again, as my dad and I run down the basketball court. He has coached my team for six years and has had no problems with the running the job requires. This has been *our thing* that we love to do together. I am grateful for God's faithfulness.

Lydia, 15

Day Four

Mary Magdalene:
A Friend to the End

Mary was from the town of Magdala, a place where the hills extend to the Lake of Galilee. She was a woman of influence and financial means. Her finely crafted clothing was a symbol of her status.

Yet, no matter how put together she appeared to be on the outside, her personal life was falling apart. She was tormented day and night by an inner gnawing that she couldn't quite explain.

She was glad she didn't have to try to explain it to Jesus. This Great Physician instantly knew the diagnosis:

Demons. Seven of them.

Though they had overpowered Mary for years, they were no match for the Son of God. With the words of his lips he cast those evil spirits out of her (see Mark 16:9).

From the moment Jesus entered her life and healed her, Mary was a faithful follower. She was devoted to him wholeheartedly. She supported his ministry with her own money. She knew first-hand that he was worth investing in (see Luke 8:1-3).

Mary's deep devotion to Jesus showed up in her actions and her attitudes. Unlike many of the others, who ran, hid, and deserted Jesus, Mary was true-blue, a friend 'til the end!

She was there at the foot of the cross. She witnessed the nailing of her Savior to the wooden beams, saw him suffocating as his lungs filled with fluid. She heard his last words, saw the soldier spear his side (see Mark 15:40).

Mary was neither afraid nor ashamed.

When Jesus was removed from the cross, she followed to see

where he was laid. Then after the Sabbath, at the crack of dawn, Mary was one of the *first* to return to the tomb with spices to use on Jesus' body. But to her amazement, the stone had been rolled away and Jesus' body was gone!

After two angels had appeared and told her that Jesus was alive, that he had risen, she ran to the others. She was the *first* to report that Jesus' tomb was empty!

Mary returned to the tomb with Peter and John who saw for themselves that her report was true. They returned to town, but Mary stayed (see Luke 24:1-12).

She was so distressed. She had to know: Who had taken him? Where had they laid his body? She couldn't keep herself from crying.

As with each of us, Jesus was nearer than she could imagine!

He stood behind her, "Woman, why are you weeping? Whom are you seeking?" he asked.

Mary never looked up—she thought it was the gardener speaking to her. Between her sobs she said, "Sir, if you have carried Him away, tell me where you have laid Him, and I will take Him away" (John 20:15, NASB).

In a voice so tender, Jesus called her by name, "Mary."

Snapping her head in the direction of the voice, she must have thought she was dreaming. But, no, there stood Jesus.

Mary Magdalene was the *first* to see the risen Savior! Jesus gave her a message to take to the others. She ran to tell them everything that had happened (see John 20:16-18).

Do you see how much Mary loved Jesus? Can you sense her sold-out devotion to him? Do you see the footprints of faithfulness throughout her story? Mary Magdalene was a faithful friend and a faithful follower of the miracle man who had changed her life. She is a perfect example of what it means to be lusciously loyal!

Beauty Builders

1. What impresses you the most about Mary Magdalene's faithfulness to the Lord? Read 1 Timothy 3:11. What do you think the world would be like without faithful women?

2. When Jesus entered Mary's life, he *became* her life. But only because she let him! Are you letting Jesus *be* your life or are you holding back? How? Why?

Day Five

Getting Personal: Which Hue Are You?

Pick up your pen, 'cause it's time to discover your color! Yep! Each color represents a different level of faithfulness. Are you true-blue, lemon-yellow, or pale-pink? Read the following situations, then choose which color best corresponds with the way you would react. X marks the spot, like this!

✗ True-blue   Yes! That's me, I'd do it.
☐ Mellow-yellow Sometimes, sorta, maybe.
☐ Pale-pink   Nah, not me, probably not.

1. It's Saturday and your dad asked you to finish raking the leaves before noon. It's 10:45 A.M., you just woke up, and you feel supergroggy. You're tempted to go back to sleep, but you get up and get raking.
☐ True-blue
☐ Mellow-yellow
☐ Pale-pink

2. You told your younger sister you'd teach her how to make a friendship bracelet this afternoon, but a friend just invited you to the mall. You stay home with your sister.
☐ True-blue
☐ Mellow-yellow
☐ Pale-pink

3. As president of the pep club, it's your responsibility to make sure all two hundred balloons are blown up before tonight's basketball game. Only one club member showed up to help. You're sort of upset, but the two of you huff and puff until the job's done.

- ☐ True-blue
- ☐ Mellow-yellow
- ☐ Pale-pink

4. You have purposed in your heart to read the Bible and write in your prayer journal regularly. So far, so good!

- ☐ True-blue
- ☐ Mellow-yellow
- ☐ Pale-pink

5. For years you have been visiting your grandma every week. She looks forward to your stories, jokes, and hugs. Even though Saturday is a big social day with your new friends, you know Grandma's waiting and you wouldn't want to let her down. It's to Grandmother's house you go!

- ☐ True-blue
- ☐ Mellow-yellow
- ☐ Pale-pink

6. Your best friend calls you at all hours of the night asking for advice. She's going through a rough time at home and she knows you'll always be there for her, no matter what time it is!

- ☐ True-blue
- ☐ Mellow-yellow
- ☐ Pale-pink

7. Sitting in church gets a bit boring at times, but you always go (with a happy attitude), because you know it pleases God (and your parents).

☐ True-blue
☐ Mellow-yellow
☐ Pale-pink

OK, what's on your palette? Count up how many X's on each color.

True-blue   _____
Mellow-yellow   _____
Pale-pink   _____

Mostly **True-blue?**
You go, girl! You are flourishing in the beautiful quality of faithfulness. Yeah, it's not always easy to be faithful, but you're making the right choices. You're proving to be dependable, loyal, committed, and determined to keep your word!

Mostly **Mellow-yellow?**
You're on your way to becoming lusciously loyal! Your heart is probably there, but your flesh is dragging you down! Why let it win? Don't let impulsiveness, laziness, tiredness, or inconvenience paint you a color you don't want to be!

Mostly **Pale-pink?**
Looking a bit washed out. Better schedule a private lesson with the Master Artist! Ask him to color your heart with HIS hues. He can help stir within you the desire to be a trustworthy, reliable, stick-to-it, kind of gorgeous gal!

There are six plain but powerful words I long to hear when I get to heaven. Guess which ones they are. Are they...

☐ Your mansion is waiting for you!

☐ Did you have a nice trip?

☐ How is the weather on earth?

☐ You're still lookin' good, old gal!

No, none of these. What I long to hear most is something very different.... *Well done, good and faithful servant.*

Yes, it will be wonderful to arrive in heaven, my real home, and to be welcomed by family and friends who arrived before me, but to see a smile on the Master's face and hear him say "Well done" is all that really matters to me.

Will God say that to everyone? Nope. Only to those who have been obedient and to those who have been faithful!

Think about it. How awesome it will be to find out that I have been the kind of woman that God himself has been able to trust! Oh, to have been dependable and loyal to the Lord! To have received assignments from God because he knew I would stick to them, see them through, not wimp out, not buckle under pressure.

To be counted faithful to share the good news of Jesus with others, to teach others the Word and to help them grow in their faith, to use for his service the spiritual gifts he has entrusted to me!

That, my dear friends, is being truly beautiful! That's what I want to be. That's the kind of beauty I want to be known for!

What about you?

What words do you want to hear when you get to heaven?

Beauty Builders

1. When is it most challenging for you to be faithful to others, to God, to yourself? Why?

2. If you were mellow-yellow or pale-pink, what could you do to become true-blue?

3. With all the firsthand knowledge you now have about faithfulness, create a plan of action.

Heavenly Father,
Thank you for your unending faithfulness to me. Thank you for being a God who can be trusted and depended upon.
Father, other people in my life break their promises, but you do not. You are a promise-keeper. You will not break your word! For that, I am grateful.
Lord, help me to be aware when the enemies of faithfulness threaten to take over. Help me to be diligent, devoted, and dependable to you, to my family, and to my friends.
Fill me with your faithfulness, that I might be lusciously loyal in all things. In Jesus' name, Amen.

Weekend Journal

Faithfulness is the point of Jesus' parable in Matthew 25:14-30. Read these words, prayerfully, taking note of the servant's actions. Then write a letter to God expressing your desire to hear the words, "Well done, good and faithful servant."

Dear Heavenly Father,

With love,

Chapter Nine

Majestically Meek!

*The Beautiful Quality
of Gentleness*

Preciously Unpretentious

"To be gentle is to be humble and tenderhearted."
Meagan, 15

She tenderly kisses the soft skin on her baby's forehead as she snuggles the child ever closer to her chest. Her warm embrace assures the child of its safety; the light stroking of the baby's fine hair communicates the deep love in her heart.

A mother caring for her child.

That is the apostle Paul's word-picture of gentleness in 1 Thessalonians 2:7. Pretty good for a guy, huh?

Gentleness is probably the most misunderstood of all the Holy Spirit's qualities. Gentleness, also known as meekness, gets trashed in our society. Meekness rhymes with weakness, but they are light-years apart. To be meek does not mean you are naive, wimpy, or spineless. Just because people are gentle does not mean they are doormats!

True gentleness is rooted in the knowledge that you are loved and accepted and valued by God. You don't have to prove yourself to anyone. No need to toot your own horn or build yourself a trophy case. You are valued by God, and that allows you to be gentle toward others.

But does being gentle mean you can't wrestle your brother or challenge your dad to a little one-on-one B-ball? Does it mean you have to be soft-spoken and boring? No, no, and no! Gentleness is referring to the condition of your *spirit*, not your personality!

Being a young woman whose spirit is full of gentleness and meekness is not only perfectly pretty, but she's also precious to God! She's of great value and worth!

Honest, and here's proof:

Be beautiful inside, in your hearts, with the lasting charm of a gentle and quiet spirit which is so precious to God.

1 PETER 3:4, TLB

Whew! If being gentle is precious to God, it must be pretty important. So let's dig deeper. Let's brainstorm! Why is a gentle spirit so special to God?

First, when you're gentle, you are responsive to God. You open yourself fully to him and allow him to work in your life. Gentleness does not push God away, but longs to be as close to him as possible.

Second, when you're gentle in spirit, you accept the uncontrollable events in your life as gifts from a God who loves you. You say "Yes, Lord" instead of "No, Lord."

Third, when you have a gentle heart, you have a grateful heart. You're thankful for who you are, what you look like, and what you own, for everything you have and everything you *don't* have!

Fourth, when you're gentle, you treat others the way God would treat them—you're caring, tender, kind, merciful, respectful, polite! That's because you're not contending to get ahead of everyone. They are not your competition; therefore you can be considerate!

Fifth, when you are genuinely gentle, you are unpretentious. You're the real thing! That's because you have a healthy perspective of yourself, and you know that your true worth comes from God.

Sixth, when a gentle attitude resides in your heart, it doesn't puff itself up. Nope! True gentleness lets God get the glory—for everything!

No wonder this beautiful quality is so precious to God. It is a rare and priceless gem in our hard-nosed, me-first world. Just think how your tantalizing tender quality of gentleness could turn the world upside down!

Beauty Builders

1. Have you ever been teased or misunderstood for being meek and gentle? How did you respond? Which of the descriptions of gentleness are most challenging to you?

2. Why do you suppose that girls who are genuinely gentle (with no hidden motives) have so many friends? Why do you think 1 Peter 3:4 calls gentleness a lasting charm?

Day Two

Pride Is Just Not Pretty

When the spotlights hit her evening gown, the sequins shimmered as if they were dancing. Her breasts had a similar effect, as she strutted her stuff during the swimsuit competition, for they were perched high from all the padding. After the talent competition, as she took her second, third, and fourth bows, she knew her acting ability had mesmerized the judges. She had them right where she wanted them!

No wonder she won the pageant.

But this girl was the epitome of pride.

She was arrogant. She was snooty. She wasn't going to let anyone or anything dash her dream of becoming a Broadway superstar. She even went so far as to get an additional phone line and created her own talent agency that managed only one client—her!

You can dress it up, but pride is just not pretty! It is the opposite of being meek and gentle. It is an attitude that eventually leaves a person friendless and alone.

Pride is arrogant—"I know what's best!"

Pride is haughty—"I would never associate with them!"

Pride is self-centered—"I am most important!"

Pride is rebellious—"I only do what I want to do!"

Notice a pattern? I, I, I, I!

That's the problem with pride. There's no room for you, me ... or even God. It is "I"-focused!

Beware of getting tangled in pride's web.

Peer into these truths about pride and humility:

- ❁ Pride leads to arguments; be humble, take advice and become wise (Proverbs 13:10, TLB).
- ❁ Pride disgusts the Lord. Take my word for it—proud men shall be punished (Proverbs 16:5, TLB).
- ❁ Pride goes before destruction and haughtiness before a fall (Proverbs 16:18, TLB).
- ❁ Better poor and humble than rich and proud (Proverbs 16:19, TLB).
- ❁ Pride ends in destruction; humility ends in honor (Proverbs 18:12, TLB).

Which one honestly requires true strength of character? Which do you think God wants to see in our lives? Pride or humility?

Humility! This beautiful quality helps us put others first and do things that will benefit them (and God). That takes true strength.

Humility also draws us into a deeper relationship with God. The psalmist shares this classified top-secret information with us. It gives us keen insight into God. Here it is: "He guides the humble in what is right and teaches them his way" (Psalm 25:9, NIV).

When we are humble before God, he teaches us more about who he is and he reveals himself to us. He guides us, shows us where to go, what to do. We develop a new intimacy with God when we are humble.

As with all the beauty qualities the Holy Spirit supplies us, humility starts with a choice. Then as you abide in the Vine and spend time with God learning his ways, humility—gentleness and meekness—becomes a true part of who you are. It's not an act. It's not a polished performance in front of a panel of judges. It's the real you. Crowned with majestic meekness!

Beauty Builders

1. Why do you think it takes a truly strong person to be humble? According to Ephesians 4:1-3, how do you think that conducting yourself with humility and gentleness is honoring to God?

2. Take a little jog over to 1 Peter 5:5-6. How does God react to the proud? To the humble? What happens—in due time—if you humble yourself before God?

Random Acts of Gentleness

Actions speak louder than words! Prove your gentleness with these:

- ✿ Tell others (especially family members) that you appreciate them.
- ✿ Pray about what to do before you do it.
- ✿ Put your arm around a troubled friend.
- ✿ Choose to cooperate and be flexible.
- ✿ Don't listen to gossip. Get to know a person for yourself!
- ✿ Say, "Please!" Otherwise it sounds like you're giving people orders, which is *not* being gentle!
- ✿ When others are trying to dig at you, keep looking at them and telling yourself, "Jesus loves them."
- ✿ Practice keeping your strength under perfect control.
- ✿ Keep quiet if your words might hurt someone else.

"Pursue righteousness, godliness, faith, love, perseverance, and gentleness."

1 TIMOTHY 6:11, NAS

Day Three

Jesus:
Gentle and Humble in Heart

Jesus is the perfect blend of all the beautiful (well, handsome in his case) qualities of the Holy Spirit. Over the past weeks together we've seen his love and joy expressed through the cross. We've seen him as the Prince of Peace and the Good Shepherd. We've seen his faithfulness through the ages to his people. Today, we'll see his gentleness and his humility.

In fact, Jesus is the extreme example of humility. He willingly laid aside his position as Prince of heaven, where he walked streets of gold and strolled along rivers of living water! He willingly kissed his Father farewell and came to earth as a human (see Philippians 2:5-7).

That, girlfriend, is humility!

But that was only the beginning.

As he walked this earth, those around him witnessed acts of gentleness and humility. I'm so glad they cared enough to record them!

Hand in hand, let's stroll through the pages of history, taking note of the gentle Lamb of God.

Ooh! It was a mob scene! Someone had caught this lowlife woman in the despicable act of adultery! She had broken her marriage vows and given in to the lusts of her flesh.

The crowd gathered around her, stones in hand, ready to fire away. But first they asked Jesus if he thought she should be killed for her sin. Jesus said that whoever was sin-free could go ahead and set sail to the first stone. No one did. They dropped their stones.

They all left. Jesus went to the woman and told her that she was forgiven, urging her to not sin again. He treated her with undeserved tenderness (see John 8:1-11).

Remember the incident with the two blind men? They had heard of the wonderful works of this miracle man and came to Jesus, asking him to have mercy on them and to heal their eyes. With the touch of his hand, their eyes were opened! And what did Jesus ask of them? "Hey fellas, please don't tell anyone, 'K?" That's humility! (see Matthew 9:27-31).

Let's wander into the Garden of Gethsemane. Jesus had been there with the disciples for several hours deep in prayer. Suddenly the Roman soldiers, the Pharisees, and the chief priests burst through the garden gates with torches and weapons. In an effort to protect his leader, Peter drew his sword and cut off the ear of the high priest's slave!

"Stop! No more of this," Jesus said. Then he reached up, touched the slave's ear, and healed him. (There's gentleness in action again!) Jesus then made it clear that he would have NO FIGHTING! He informed them all that if he needed to be rescued he only needed to call out to the Father and he would be surrounded with thousands of angels! But, no. In peace, gentleness, and humility, Jesus willingly surrendered and walked the road to Calvary (see Matthew 26:47-56; Luke 22:47-53).

Jesus' great strength was submitted to the will of God. That is meekness. Not weakness. That's the height of humility. That's our Jesus!

Beauty Builders

1. Read Jesus' autobiographical statement in Matthew 11:28-30. How can you learn to be extra gentle and mildly meek from Jesus' example?

2. Check out Philippians 2:3-4. List the three instructions given in these verses. How do you think each of these can help you become more Christlike?

Day Four

Miriam's Motto: Anything Mo' Can Do, I Can Do Better!

Most of us go through seasons when it seems harder to behave the way the Holy Spirit wants us to behave! Have you ever had *one of those days* when your good intentions turned sour, or your desire to be loyal took a left turn?

Miriam can relate.

Overall, she had lived a godly life.

As a seven-year-old, she courageously stood guard over the basket that hid her baby brother Moses in the reeds. With poise and politeness she approached the Pharaoh's daughter, who had discovered Moses, and asked if she wanted her to get a Hebrew woman to nurse the baby for her. Miriam returned with her mother—Moses' *real* mom!

With Moses now in the Pharaoh's palace, Miriam spent years and years gently and confidently encouraging her fellow Hebrew people that God would deliver them from the taskmaster hand of Pharaoh. She knew God was going to use Moses to do this! Moses was God's chosen leader!

The day finally arrived. The day of escape from Egypt, the day to witness the mighty hand of God. The sea parted and the Hebrew people crossed it on dry land. A miracle!

Miriam grabbed her timbrel and the hand of a friend and she led the women in a song of rejoicing, in a dance of jubilee! (See Exodus 15:21.) Her heart was full of gratitude toward the Lord, and she wanted to express it openly.

But a few years later there was something else she expressed openly—her opinion about Moses' new wife. Yep. That was the day of downfall! The day we see Miriam having *one of those days.* The day when the beautiful qualities of gentleness and meekness ran dry!

Moses tied the knot with a Cushite (non-Hebrew) woman, a woman who had not been raised as one of God's chosen people (see Numbers 12:1).

Miriam had a little problem with this. OK, a *big* problem with this! She did not want this woman as Moses' wife, to be elevated and esteemed above herself. After all, she was one of God's chosen people, the Israelites. She didn't exactly welcome the woman into the family with open arms. The only thing she opened her arms to was pride.

I can just see the dust flying as she stamped her feet. After giving an earful to her brother Aaron, she reasoned that they could do without Moses. "Has the Lord spoken only through Moses? ... Hasn't he also spoken through us?" (Numbers 12:2, NIV).

She openly criticized Moses and challenged his authority. Pride had gotten the best of her. Could she have thought she could lead the people just as well as Moses had? Did she really believe that Moses should step down for marrying this Cushite woman? Was she willing to cause a tiff in her family as well as her nation?

Yep. Probably so.

But there was someone of even greater importance than Miriam or Moses! Someone who was eavesdropping on her.

God.

Gulp.

The Lord called a private powwow with Miriam, Moses, and Aaron. He got on Miriam's case big time for criticizing Moses, his chosen leader, the most humble man who had ever lived. Then he nipped her pride in the bud—right there, right then.

God humbled her with a bad case of leprosy. Drastic? Yes. Effective? Oh, yes.

Yet, Moses, the meek and gentle one, did not hold a grudge against his sister. He cried out to the Lord, "Heal her, O God, I beg you!" (Numbers 12:13, TLB).

And he did. After seven days!

Tough way to learn a lesson. A prideful, harsh spirit is not honoring to the Lord. I doubt Miriam struggled with pride after that. I would suspect that as one of Israel's leading ladies, she returned to being a gentle and grateful woman.

Beauty Builders

1. Why do you think God honored Moses' humble attitude and punished Miriam's pride?

2. Have you ever felt threatened by someone the way Miriam did? How did you react? How can pride mess up our relationships and cause us to behave rudely?

Gorgeous Girl Profile
My Hero, My Mom

*Listen to these true stories about two moms whose gentle manner—
even under pressure or in spite of persecution—glorified God and won
the respect of their daughters.*

Just the other night after feeling overwhelmed by life, my mom
reminded me once again not to place my eyes on what surrounds
me, but to place them on our mighty God. She doesn't just say
this, she lives it. Her faith in God has never been affected by the
waves that have crashed around her. Instead, time after time, I've
seen her stretch her hand out to Jesus and walk toward him on the
water (figuratively, of course). She remains loving, gentle, strong,
and encouraging. Her faith in God, and in me, never falters. She is
my hero and I love her so!

Lindy, 18

My mother moved from Colombia, South America, to the United
States, when she was nineteen. She struggled for fifteen years as a
single mom raising my brother and me. There was no sacrifice she
wasn't willing to make … it is as though no trace of selfishness
dwelt in her.

Sometimes people look down on my mother because she is not
an articulate, all-American woman with fancy clothes and influen-
tial friends. She gets treated differently at stores, my school, and
over the phone. It always makes me furious.

I'm grateful God opened my heart and eyes to realize how *he*
sees my mother. She is the image of Christlike love, morality, and
goodness. I only ask the Lord to create a tender love and gentle
nature like hers in me. Then I will have everything!

Stephanie, 17

Day Five

Getting Personal:
Do You Answer With Empathy?

Gentle answers. Gentle actions. When these attributes are combined, they make a young woman absolutely awesome. The two make her glow with a beauty from within. They make it evident that she is abiding in Christ and allowing his Spirit to flow through her!

That's because gentleness comes through in her understanding, tenderhearted, and meek responses. The gentle young woman is empathetic.

No, no, not to be mixed up with pathetic or apathetic!

To be *empathetic* means you have the ability to step into others' shoes, to imagine living in their skin and experiencing what they are experiencing. This helps you to be more sensitive to what they are thinking and feeling. Therefore, you will respond to them with greater understanding. You will respond with true gentleness.

Let's explore the idea of empathy. Let's take an empathy exam to see how well you communicate understanding in a gentle manner.

Answering With Empathy

Select the answers that communicate understanding and respond with gentleness!

1. *"I detest chemistry, and I just know I'm going to bomb this test."*
   a. "Oh, stop it! You always do great."
   b. "You sound concerned. I'll bet you'll do fine."

2. *"My mom is having a biopsy today on a lump in her breast."*
   a. "She is? You must be scared."
   b. "Really? That sounds gross. I'll bet it will really hurt. I hope she's not going to die."

3. *"I hate my brother. He's a total jerk."*
   a. "I like your brother. He's always nice to me, besides he's so cute."
   b. "Sounds like you two are having some problems. What's up?"

4. *"Hey, look, I got a B+ on my English paper!"*
   a. "Way to go. I know how hard you worked on it."
   b. "Cool. I got an A."

5. *"My family is going camping over spring break."*
   a. "You mean you're spending your whole vacation sleeping on the ground? We're going on a cruise."
   b. "Back to nature, huh? Sounds fun."

6. *"Jason just made fun of me for wearing baggy clothes."*
   a. "That must have hurt. But, hey, God likes it better than that skin-tight stuff."
   b. "Well, you do look sort of dumpy."

7. *"I sat behind Jenny in class today. She's so thin! I feel totally huge! I think I'll skip lunch today."*
   a. "That's a good start, but you'll have to skip more than lunch to look like her."
   b. "Next to her, a pencil looks fat! I think you look great."

8. *"You always qualify for our forensic debates."*
   a. "I know you're really trying your best. Do you think I could help you in some way?"
   b. "Yep, and I've done it all on my own."

   Scoring is simple!
   Give yourself 100 points for each correct answer.
   1. b   2. a   3. b   4. a   5. b   6. a   7. b   8. a

600–800 pointss: Yeah! You are very understanding and know how to answer with gentleness.

300–500 points: Keep trying! Put yourself in their situation and respond from there.

0–200 points: You selected the harshest, least understanding answers. Better back up and get a grasp on gentle before someone gets a grasp on you!

   Our gentle way of responding to others communicates that we care. It shows that we are secure in our relationship with God, knowing our true value comes from him.

Beauty Builders

1. What aspect of gentleness is hardest for you to express?

2. What changes do you need to make in your attitudes, your actions, and your life to be able to grace others with gentleness?

3. Based on all you've learned this week about gentleness, meekness, and humility, create a plan of action.

Heavenly Father,
I ask that by your Spirit, you would grant me the ability to put myself in the place of others—to see and feel their needs—and to respond to them with a humble heart. Lord, I desire to be a young woman filled with your gentle Spirit, to be found precious in your sight. Keep me from being prideful and self-focused. As a daughter of the King (that's you!), grant me the gentle grace to be majestically meek. In Jesus' name, Amen.

Weekend Journal

Write a letter to God expressing your desire to become just like Jesus—who described himself as gentle and humble in heart.

Dear Heavenly Father,

With love,

_____

Chapter Ten

Radiantly Restrained!

*The Beautiful Quality
of Self-Control*

Get a Grip on Yourself!

"Self-control is the ability to say no to the wrong things and yes to the right things."
Katie, 16

W hat I do and what I want to do are two different things. If we all just went around doing whatever we wanted, there would be chaos."

That's my favorite quote of Simon's from the movie *Simon Birch*. It defines our final beautiful quality so clearly! Self-control is keeping ourselves from doing and saying things that would be ungodly or displeasing to our heavenly Father. It means putting ourselves under the control of the Holy Spirit. We may *want* to do something wrong, but we don't!

Simon is right that if we all just went around doing whatever we wanted without regard to others or God, the world would be chaotic. Actually, that's sort of how it is! The world we live in is Satan's playground. Most people *do* do whatever they want.

But not us! Not those who love God and are called according to his purpose and his plan.

I asked the Lord over and over how I could best describe the concept of self-control. Here it is:

The beautiful qualities of the Holy Spirit are like that adorable little Toyota Jeep—RAV4! (Stay with me here!)

Love is the gas! It is the fuel. It is the motivation in the life of a Christian.

The next seven beautiful qualities represent all the places we want to go and the things we want to see in our four-wheel-drive jeep!

But without self-control, we'll never get there!

Yep! You guessed it!

Self-control is the steering wheel!

It's only when self-control is guiding us, that we will love the unlovely, have joy in a whirlwind of sorrow, trust God to the point of feeling at peace, patiently wait on others, reach out in kindness, choose to do what's morally good, remain faithful when we want to quit, and be genuinely gentle and humble, even if we have just cause not to!

OK, we've got gas and we know where we want to go; the steering wheel is ready.

So how do we get this Jeep jumpin'?

The key to starting the engine is submission. There's that big, heavy word! It just implies that we are to line up our will to God's will. That's the *self* part of self-control. It is us choosing to submit our desires, emotions, urges, temptations, and lusts to the control of the Holy Spirit. (Some people think self-control means that you're in charge! You call the shots. Nope! That's the Holy Spirit's job.)

It could more accurately be called "control over our self"—specifically our *old* self. Our flesh. Remember our little chat about the flesh back in chapter one? Our sinful flesh declares war on our new self, our new nature that is godly.

First Peter 4:1-5 tells us to spend the rest of the time we have in the flesh (in our bodies) no longer doing crummy things like using people, getting drunk, lying and cheating, being sexually immoral, and selfish (just to name a few).

But don't worry! You don't do it alone! Once you choose to

submit your will to God, the Holy Spirit moves in and gives you the power to put the pedal to the metal and start cruisin' in style!

Yes, there may be some rough terrain ahead, but after awhile, you're gonna just love riding around town in the Jeep! And when you're tempted to take the wrong exit, you'll know exactly what to do!

Beauty Builders

1. Set your eyes on 1 Peter 4:1-5. Which of the fleshly desires do you have the hardest time controlling? Write a prayer asking the Holy Spirit to pour his power into you so that he can have total control.

2. Do you ever get discouraged when your self-control seems to be slipping? Don't get discouraged, get angry! At whom? Read 1 Peter 5:8. Who's trying to run your Jeep off the road? What can you do to protect yourself?

Day Two

Tackling the Big T

Derek finally asked Darcy to the prom. For months she'd been hoping it would happen. She already knew which dress at Macy's would make her look smashing! Let's see, she wanted her hair twisted up, her nails manicured, and a touch of glitter on the tops of her cheeks! She was completely prepared. Except for prom night itself when they were alone in Derek's car. His sweet kisses were melting her fears and inhibitions. When his hand slowly began to move up the front of her dress, she tried to block out the little voice telling her to stop him.

* * *

Kimmy had spent extra time praying today, because she had so many decisions facing her. Mr. Francis needed her to tell him if she was going to accept the position as president of FFA. Of course, she really wanted to tell her best friend Laura that she'd go out for track with her. Plus, she almost forgot, Pastor Jim asked her to pray about leading devotions at the youth camp out, which was the only thing she really felt God leading her to do. But by the end of the day, she was really in a tangled mess. She told Mr. Francis yes! She told Laura yes! She told Pastor Jim yes!

* * *

All of Abby's friends were going. They didn't tell their parents and didn't seem to be suffering for it. But Abbie was sweating bullets. She knew her mom drew the line on R-rated movies. But she couldn't bear to tell her friends she couldn't go. As she bought the ticket for the PG-rated flick, she wondered how they were going to sneak over to the R and not get caught.

Darcy, Kimmy, and Abbie all needed the same thing! Self-control!

Darcy needed to stick to her standards even though she liked Derek and had waited forever for this special night. It was not the time to be uninhibited and allow her crush to crunch her self-control.

Kimmy needed to be able to say no to the things that God was not leading her to do. Being undisciplined was complicating her life!

Abbie knew better than to lie to her mom and sneak into a raunchy movie. But she felt the pressure of her peers and wanted to be counted as one of the group. Unfortunately, tossing her morals to the wind was bound to land her in a tornado!

One thing that would help each of these girls have the self-control they need is to know how to resist the big T. Temptation!

Temptation is Satan's biggest weapon. Here are some temptation-tackling tips for dodging his fiery darts the next time he shoots them your way.

- ✿ *Be 100 percent sold-out to following Christ.* Determine to give him first place in every area of life (see Colossians 1:18).

- ✿ *Study the Word!* When Jesus was tempted by Satan after forty days in the desert, he used the Scriptures to fight off Satan's half-truths and temptations (see Matthew 4:1-11).

- ✿ *Be committed to prayer.* In the Garden of Gethsemane Jesus told the disciples to stay alert and pray in order to resist temptation. The spirit is willing, but the flesh is weak (see Matthew 26:41).

- ✿ *Call on God's power to strengthen you!* Remember he lives within you, and he is mightier than the enemy (see 1 Corinthians 6:19-20; 1 John 4:4).

- ✿ *Watch for a way of escape!* God says you won't be tempted beyond what you can take without his opening a way for you to get out (see 1 Corinthians 10:13).

✿ *Don't put yourself in compromising situations.* Think ahead! (see Proverbs 13:16).

✿ *Hang with friends who love God and share your values.* The wrong friends will pull you down (see 1 Corinthians 15:33).

Keep these tips tucked inside your heart! When Satan tries to tempt you, the Spirit of God—and you—will be ready to take him on!

It really *does* matter what we do! Our minds and bodies often want to trick us into thinking that no one will ever know, or it won't make any difference if we do whatever we want—whenever we want. Wrong! God has given us self-control for a reason!

Beauty Builders

1.Do you identify with Darcy's, Kim's, or Abbie's situation? How could self-control make a difference in each of their lives?

2. When you resist Satan by obeying God's Word, how does he react? Read James 4:7 and fill in the blanks.

_____ therefore to _____. Resist the devil and he will _____ from you.

Random Acts of Self-Control

Ready for some ways to restrain yourself? Keep reading!

✿ Team up with a friend who will lovingly confront you when you blow it.

✿ Know your weak spots, your temptations, and where you're likely to sin. Then stay away!

✿ Don't keep looking at the wrong things, like fashion magazines and romance novels.

✿ Set standards! Set boundaries! This will help you keep them.

✿ When you get angry or feel like making a sarcastic remark, bite your tongue—literally!

✿ Don't be afraid to stand alone. That may encourage others to join you!

✿ Remain responsible, even when others do not.

✿ Remember that being a role model is hard, but it may influence someone's life for Christ.

✿ Every choice carries consequences! Think things through before each decision.

✿ Use sound judgment! Avoid falling for the if-it-feels-good-do-it lie.

Finally, be strong in the Lord and in his mighty power.

EPHESIANS 6:10, NIV

Day Three

Jesus: Warrior With a Secret Weapon

It may have been the longest, most exhausting few weeks of Jesus' life.

He had gone without food the entire time—perhaps he was dreaming of his first bite of pizza, a taco, or a chilidog. This food-free trip had left him weak and very tired. Oh, for a Power Bar! This was definitely not a good time to have his self-control tested!

He had spent forty days in the wilderness region of Judea. Boring. Barren. But quiet! He was alone the whole time—well, except for the dastardly deceiver who kept trying to trick him into sinning.

Satan. The Father of Lies. The evil one. The nerve of that sly guy! Jesus had just been baptized in the Jordan River by his cousin John the Baptist and had witnessed a true phenomenon. When he came up out of the water, the heavens opened up. God spoke to him and sent the Holy Spirit down to fill him for the mission ahead of him.

It was a spiritual high!

Satan didn't waste any time. He moved right in to attack! He had one goal in mind: GET THIS GUY TO BLOW IT! Tempt him and get him to sin against his God!

Of course, all of this was part of God's plan. He was overseeing the entire operation. Jesus *had* to be tempted by Satan. Temptation is part of being human, and Jesus needed to face the same human temptations we face and overcome them, to prove to us it can be done. And, to prove he was truly God's Son and qualified to be the King of the World, the Savior of our souls.

Therefore, he had to be tempted; he had to be proven sinless.

Satan gave it his best shot. He knew Jesus was hungry, so he tempted him with fresh, hot bread! Jesus' response: "No! For the Scriptures tell us that bread won't feed men's souls: obedience to every word of God is what we need" (Matthew 4:4, TLB).

So Satan tried to get him to jump off the top of the temple in Jerusalem. After all, the Scriptures said God would send angels to rescue him.

Jesus' response: "It also says not to put the Lord your God to a foolish test!" (v. 7).

Satan tried a new angle. He took Jesus to the top of a mountain and told him that he would give Jesus the whole world and all its glory, if he would bow down and worship at Satan's feet! He offered Jesus power and worldly wealth.

Jesus' response: "Get out of here, Satan,... The Scriptures say, 'Worship only the Lord God. Obey only him'" (v. 10).

OK, fine! Satan was outta there, with his tail between his legs. A whipped puppy! Jesus did not bite the bait. He did not yield to temptation; he did not sin. He exercised self-control.

Did you notice what weapon Jesus used to fight Satan? The Word of God! He drew it out like a sword and cut Satan down to size.

God's Word—knowing it and doing it—is *our* weapon, too! (see Ephesians 6:17). It will give us the self-control we need, no matter what situation we face. It's the power we need when our defenses are down and we're rationalizing ("Oh, it's just a little white lie, who will know?") or ready to compromise ("Well, I just won't let him go *all* the way").

Count on the Holy Spirit's presence, speak out God's promises from his Word, and self-control will be yours. Jesus showed us the way! Let's follow his lead.

Beauty Builders

1. Was Jesus really tempted by the same things that tempt us? Did he use self-control every time? Find out in Hebrews 4:15-16! How does knowing this help you?

2. Satan tries to tempt us in the same three ways he tempted Jesus. They are clearly defined in 1 John 2:15-16. In which of these areas do you need the most self-control?

Day Four

Rahab Leaves Her Past Behind

Have you ever been in a situation where you gave in and did the wrong thing because at the time you couldn't see any other way out of a situation?

Rahab did!

She was a single woman living in the great city of Jericho. She was an innkeeper, working hard to keep her business open. Perhaps that's why she turned to prostitution. Certainly it wasn't a decision she was proud of. It showed no self-control. Nevertheless, she sold her body to the men of the city and to the travelers who came through town.

It wasn't unusual for strange men to come knocking on the door of her inn. But the two men who had just arrived seemed a bit odd. Indeed they were! They were spies, Salmon and Joab, from the army of Israel who had been sent in to check out the city, which Joshua, their leader, had plans to attack and conquer.

Rahab had heard of the God of Israel. The way he parted the Red Sea, the way he was leading his people into battle all across the land! Rahab knew Joshua and his army were headed her way. She was not afraid. She believed the God of Israel to be the one true God.

So, without hesitation, she hid the two spies on her rooftop, underneath the flax she had laid out to dry. She risked her life to protect theirs!

When the king's men came looking for the spies, she admitted they had been there, but said they had left.

In exchange for protecting the spies, Rahab asked that she and her entire family would be spared in the battle against Jericho. When the spies agreed, she lowered them down the back wall of her house with a scarlet cord, and they escaped to the mountains. The same scarlet cord, hanging from her window on the day of battle, alerted the army as to her whereabouts.

The spies kept their promise. After Joshua and his men marched around Jericho seven times, they blew the ram's horn and let out a war cry! The walls around the city instantly began to fall, and the battle began!

The entire city and all the people were wiped out, except for Rahab and her family. Though they had to live outside the camp of Israel, Rahab considered herself one of God's chosen people. In her heart she knew he was real and that he alone had spared her life (see Joshua 2, 6).

And what a great, new life it would be. Rahab had made the decision to leave her former livelihood behind her. No longer a prostitute, but a servant of the most high God.

Rahab finally exercised the self-control that was needed to live a godly life. She is an example of how beautiful a life can become when it radiates with restraint, when it blossoms with the beautiful quality of self-control.

Beauty Builders

1. Share about a time when you lacked self-control. What were the results? What would you have done differently?

Day Five

Getting Personal:
Are You Diggin' Divine Discipline?

Every single day you are given opportunities to use self-control. And every day you either choose to discipline yourself or do whatever feels good at the given moment.

Since self-control is the steering wheel that gets you where you want to go, let's take a little driving test to see where you are and where you are headed.

Use the following scale to rate yourself for each question:

1= Absolutely NO WAY

2=Not likely

3=50/50 chance

4=Likely

5=Absolutely YES

___ 1. Even though you spill your bottle of nail polish on your new skirt, you keep yourself from swearing.

___ 2. Jay is quarterback on the football team and very fine to look at, but he's known for his *moves* off the football field. He asks you out; you say no.

___ 3. All the girls at school are wearing those rib-tight tops that get the guys' attention, except you.

___ 4. Instead of letting your revengeful thoughts about your two-faced friend run wild, you choose to think of all her good points.

___ 5. You think Sunday school is dull and your youth pastor is boring, but you go anyway.

___ 6. You avoid movies, magazine, TV shows, and books that you know won't have a positive, godly influence on you.

___ 7. You're not in the mood to go to work (or school) today, but you resist the urge to call in sick.

___ 8. A daily quiet time to pray and read God's Word are a regular thing for you.

___ 9. You know it's important to be around positive examples and Christians, so you select your close friends carefully.

___ 10. Even though you want a new backpack, you use the $30 your mom gave you to buy new undergarments per her request.

___ 11. You're feeling unsure as you file into class to take your SATs, but you keep your eyes on your own answer form.

___ 12. You know family relationships are important, so you forgive when you'd rather hold a grudge.

___ 13. You're trying to eat healthier, so for lunch you choose yogurt over a cheeseburger.

___ 14. You understand your body is the home of the Holy Spirit, so you do not abuse it with drugs, alcohol, or cigarettes.

___ 15. Today's your day to work out. You're really dragging, but you go for it anyway and do your best.

___ **Your TOTAL score**

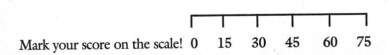

Mark your score on the scale! 0   15   30   45   60   75

50–75: Way to go, beautiful babe! You passed the test and will be awarded a driver's license! Yes, you are restraining yourself in the right situations, and when you slip, you know it! Your efforts to control yourself and please the Lord will be rewarded. Keep it up.

25–45: Caught ya! You're running a few red lights! Instead of stopping, you're racing on ahead and leaving discipline in the dust! Slow down, think each situation through. Proceed with caution.

0–20: OK, it's back to driver's ed for you! You've missed a few basic rules of the road. Refuse to be swayed by the driving habits of others. Keep studying the manual (the Bible). It will give you clear direction on when to stop, go, or yield. Without self-control, your life will constantly be in a traffic jam! Team up with an adult mentor who can help hold you accountable for wrong turns.

The cool thing about the quality of self-control is that it is a team effort between you and the Holy Spirit. You have to choose to do the right thing (God doesn't force us to do anything). Then the Holy Spirit gives you the ability to do it! It's super Spirit-power, not just your personal willpower. Willpower fails, Spirit-power prevails!

The Holy Spirit surging through you and me will help us do the things God has called us to do. Sometimes we feel like we *can't* be kind or loving or hold our tongues or keep from being angry. But the good news is that when we are weak, then he can be strong through us!

Self-control and self-discipline are an important part of living godly, holy lives. Holy means to be "set apart." We are set apart from the ways of the world to be used by God. When the beautiful qualities of love, joy, peace, patience, kindness, goodness, faithfulness, gentleness, and self-control are evident in our lives, others will know we love the Lord and are filled with his Holy Spirit.

That, girlfriend, makes you a **true beauty!**

Beauty Builders

1. In what area of your life do you find it most difficult to maintain self-control?

2. What changes could you make in your life that would help you strengthen your self-control?

3. Based on all you've learned this week about self-control, create a plan of action.

Heavenly Father,
I desire to be 100 percent sold out to you, to live for you 24/7, and to obey your Word. But I can't do it without your Holy Spirit giving me the self-control I need. So, Holy Spirit, I ask you to fill me up, from head to toe! Always show me the way to go and help me resist the temptations that Satan dangles in front of me.

I'm so grateful to know that when I do blow it and sin, you are faithful to forgive me the moment I confess it to you. And that I never lose my potential to be awesomely attractive! In Jesus' name, Amen.

Weekend Journal

Write a letter to the Lord expressing your feelings about the struggle to always do the right thing. Then ask the Holy Spirit to strengthen your desire to obey God and his Word and to fill you with the control you need to say no to anything that is not pleasing or glorifying to God.

Dear Heavenly Father,

With love,

_____

Seminars and Retreats Available
with Andrea Stephens

I'm Glad You Know Where We're Going, Lord!
Discovering God's direction in your life.

God Thinks You're Positively Awesome!
Teaching girls to love their looks!

You Want Me to W-W-W-Witness?
Learn how easy it is to tell others about Christ every day!

Being God's Kids in a Tough Teen World
*Uncover the secret of putting God first
in four important areas of your life!*

Stressed Out, but Hangin' Tough!
*Find out God's answer for handling stress,
plus tons of practical tips!*

The Importance of Being You!
*Learn how to boost your self-esteem and apprecite
your unique personality, gifts, and talents!*

Glamour to Glory:
From Model to Minister's Wife
Andrea Stephen's personal testimony

For more information contact:
Andrea Stephens
P.O. Box 2856
Bakersfield, CA 93303